THE LAND AND PEOPLE OF ISRAEL

The Portraits of the Nations Series

THE LAND AND PEOPLE OF TURKEY
BY WILLIAM SPENCER

THE LAND AND PEOPLE OF SCOTLAND
BY FREDA M. BUCHANAN

THE LAND AND PEOPLE OF GERMANY
BY RAYMOND A. WOHLRABE AND WERNER KRUSCH

THE LAND AND PEOPLE OF BELGIUM
BY DOROTHY LODER

THE LAND AND PEOPLE OF AUSTRIA
BY RAYMOND A. WOHLRABE AND WERNER KRUSCH

THE LAND AND PEOPLE OF THE PHILIPPINES
BY JOSEPHINE BUDD VAUGHAN

THE LAND AND PEOPLE OF SPAIN
BY DOROTHY LODER

THE LAND AND PEOPLE OF SOUTH AFRICA
BY ALAN PATON

THE LAND AND PEOPLE OF AUSTRALIA
BY GODFREY BLUNDEN

THE LAND AND PEOPLE OF IRELAND
BY ELINOR O'BRIEN

THE LAND AND PEOPLE OF GREECE
BY THEODORE GIANAKOULIS

THE LAND AND PEOPLE OF JAPAN
BY JOSEPHINE BUDD VAUGHAN

THE LAND OF THE ITALIAN PEOPLE
BY FRANCES WINWAR

THE LAND AND PEOPLE OF MEXICO
BY ELSA LARRALDE

THE LAND AND PEOPLE OF ISRAEL
BY GAIL HOFFMAN

THE LAND AND PEOPLE OF SWEDEN
BY FREDERIC C. NANO

THE LAND AND PEOPLE OF CANADA
BY FRANCES AILEEN ROSS

THE LAND OF THE ENGLISH PEOPLE
BY ALICIA STREET

THE LAND AND PEOPLE OF BRAZIL
BY ROSE BROWN

THE LAND OF THE POLISH PEOPLE
BY ERIC P. KELLY

THE LAND AND THE PEOPLE OF INDIA
BY MANORAMA MODAK

THE LAND OF THE CHINESE PEOPLE
BY CORNELIA SPENCER

THE LAND OF THE RUSSIAN PEOPLE
BY ALEXANDER NAZAROFF

THE LAND OF WILLIAM OF ORANGE
BY ADRIAAN J. BARNOUW

THE LAND OF WILLIAM TELL
BY LILLIAN J. BRAGDON

THE LAND OF JOAN OF ARC
BY LILLIAN J. BRAGDON

THE LAND AND PEOPLE
OF ISRAEL

BY

Gail Hoffman

PORTRAITS OF THE NATIONS SERIES

J. B. Lippincott Company
Philadelphia & New York

Library of Congress catalog card number 55-7770

CONTENTS

ILLUSTRATIONS

(in this order, following page 62)

7

AUTHOR'S NOTE

As this new edition goes to press, close to seven years have elapsed since the State of Israel has taken its place in the family of nations. Despite many difficulties, this land of freedom and democracy has made remarkable progress. Agricultural settlement and economic development have made big strides, accompanied by educational and scientific advances.

Its people have welcomed nearly a million newcomers from every part of the globe, most of them fleeing from poverty and persecution. These new settlers, like the early immigrants to the United States, brought a rich variety of traditions and qualities, new energies, and faith.

Foremost among the difficulties encountered by Israel has been the sharp hostility of eight Arab states nearby. Despite Israel's willingness to enter into the constructive relationships of peace, the Arabs have refused to discuss terms for any peace treaties. The armistice agreements have remained in force, but hundreds of border incidents increase tensions from time to time.

Palestine, the Land of Israel, has been partitioned, with the State of Israel occupying the greater part of the territory west of the River Jordan. Although the remainder is now held by Jordan and Egypt, its political future has not been definitely determined.

The Old City of Jerusalem (adjoining the new city), Bethlehem, Jericho, Hebron and Nablus lie beyond the present borders of the State of Israel. Yet no story of the Land of Israel is complete without mention of these famous Biblical landmarks, and it is best to consider the geographic formations of the country as a whole. I am hopeful that, eventually, a spirit of cooperation will minimize border barriers so that all roads will become accessible.

January 1, 1955   *Gail Hoffman*

CHAPTER ONE

A New Era in an Ancient Land

⎍⎍⎍⎍⎍⎍⎍⎍⎍⎍⎍⎍⎍⎍⎍⎍⎍⎍⎍⎍

PALESTINE, the fabulous country which has provided the setting for the best-loved dramas of all time, has come to life again after remaining silent and remote for many centuries.

It makes an amazing story. It seems almost as if the land of Israel had lain buried under piles of shifting sands and crumbling terraces—awaiting the magic touch of her returning children, whose love and devotion to her never wavered throughout two thousand years of exile.

With Walt-Disney-like rapidity, the desert dunes have sprouted towns and villages. Swampy wastelands have become fertile valleys, dotted here and there with red-tiled houses in rows and circles. Stony hillsides are blossoming with orchards and vineyards. Modern machines throb in factories and workshops. Along with the toil and the industry, new forward-looking patterns of living have been evolved.

The new State of Israel, proclaimed on May 14, 1948, is a remarkable fulfillment of an ancient dream, blended with modern social and economic plans. The strength of the movement for the return to Zion lay in the fact that it was a spontaneous reaction of the Jewish masses to a deep, long-felt need.

Exactly where is this Land of the Bible? Lying at the crossroads of the world, it forms the connecting link between three continents—Europe, Asia, and Africa. Transcontinental airlines, railways, trucks, buses and cars traverse its narrow borders. Ships of all nations come to its ports, bringing and taking their cargoes.

Look at a map of the world, and you will find that a line drawn due east from Los Angeles crosses the United States, the Atlantic Ocean, the northern hump of Africa, the eastern part of the Mediterranean Sea, and then strikes Jerusalem. The sere brown hills of southern California lie in the same degree of latitude as the buff-colored mountains of Judea!

Israel, like California, has a special kind of glorious, life-giving sunshine, month after month of cloudless blue skies. No rain falls for at least half the year. Both have the right kind of sandy soil for citrus groves. The growers of golden oranges in Pardess Hanna, Israel, believe their fruit is the finest in the world—exactly as do the growers of golden oranges in Santa Ana, California.

The ancient "Land of Promise" and the new "Land of Opportunity" have more in common than is generally realized. Young and old, from all sections of the world, have been making Israel their goal in search of work and happiness. Young and old, from all parts of the United States, have been flocking to California for the same reason.

Tel Aviv, Israel's largest city, has replaced empty sand dunes. Los Angeles, California's largest city, was built on a semi-desert too. Irrigation is bringing fertility to the soil and prosperity to the inhabitants of the Jordan Valley of Israel. Water, brought to California's Imperial Valley, is doing the same thing.

Of course, there are striking differences also. California makes you constantly aware of present-day America. Palestine never permits you to forget her past history and traditions.

To those who are familiar with the Bible—and it is the world's greatest inspiration as well as best-selling book, translated into two thousand languages and dialects—Palestine is a place that deeply stirs thoughts and emotions. As soon as you set foot in the Holy Land, you pause a moment and say to yourself—almost reverently: "Ah, here is Palestine! The Land of the Bible. The Land of Israel. From here came the concept of one God and one world in which all men are brothers. On one of these mountaintops is Jerusalem!"

Something about the scenery of the Holy Land imparts a sense of destiny, gives rise to an exaltation of the spirit. It was not by chance that the poets and prophets of the Bible poured forth their psalms of praise, hymns of thanksgiving, and exhortations to righteousness from these hills and valleys.

The seeker after spectacular beauty will find unusual combinations of land, water, and sky when he sees a full rainbow spanning the magical silence of the Dead Sea, when he catches a sudden vista of the turquoise waters of Lake Tiberias against purple-tinted mountains at sunset, and when he witnesses day breaking over the peaceful valley of northern Galilee, with Lake Huleh close by, surrounded by the Hills of Naphthali, and majestic, snow-covered Mt. Hermon towering in the distance.

Visitors who view the land in July or August in its drab bareness, after the hot sun has shone unremittingly for months, find it difficult to picture the green freshness of the landscape on a Spring morning. In February and March the hills and dales from Dan to Beersheba are clad with waving fields of wheat and barley. Each terrace and valley that has been scratched with even a primitive plow sends up green shoots, and wildflowers appear in surprising variety and profusion.

The bright red anemone is the first harbinger of the gay season, and the short-stemmed variety fills the nooks and crannies of soil-eroded hills, and carpets the plains. The annual mystery of hidden seeds and bulbs springing to life after the first rains of November, comes with something of the special effect of sunshine in rainy England. To pick wild tulips in the valleys near Ein Karim, to hunt for rose-amethyst cyclamens among the rocks of the Jerusalem hills, to gather armfuls of blue lupins, yellow jonquils, and purple hyacinths in Galilee, and to find the fields of Sharon splashed white with daisies and crimson with poppies, are experiences that leave you breathless with their shock of loveliness after six months of bleak dryness.

Moonlight is so brilliant that you can read a book or tell time by it. It floods the mountains and vales with a gleaming radiance. If you are fortunate enough to be on the summit of Mt. Tabor on a moonlit night, you can see almost the whole of Israel spread out before you with contours softened and deepened.

The Land of Israel is a surprisingly tiny country, rimming the Mediterranean Sea for only a hundred and fifty miles, from Lebanon in the north to Egypt in the south, and varying in width from twenty to seventy miles, with Jordan forming its eastern neighbor. Israel is so small that you can motor through it in a day, and yet its historical landmarks and its scenic features are so varied that you can live there for years without seeing them all. If you should want frequent changes in environment, you could find a different century and climate for each day in the week!

To history-hungry eyes, the Biblical scenes are most satisfying. Near Beersheba, a sheikh sits in the doorway of his tent, just as did the Patriarch Abraham when he saw the three visitors approaching and ran to welcome them. The sheikh's greeting, his appearance, and his hospitality have not changed from those of his famous prototype. In the Negev district in the south of Israel, men still buy plots of land, haggle over the use of wells, and kill a sheep or goat to prepare a feast for honored guests in much the same fashion as in the days of Abraham, Isaac, and Jacob.

In some of the villages, Arab women in long black dresses, colorfully embroidered, go to the well to draw water and carry it home in clay jars perched on their heads. The women of Nazareth still obtain their supply from the public fountain, as the boy Jesus must have watched his mother do. In Nazareth, too, the carpenters may be found working busily in the archways of their small shops—open to the sun. Their methods are similar to those used by Joseph and Jesus. The very houses, with walls of rough-dressed stone, domed over with clay mortar, resemble the homes of the first century. The interiors, with raised masonry platform, on which sleep the family at night, and below which gather the sheep, goats, and chickens, show little signs of change.

Haifa, Israel's chief port, is a shining example of what vision, enterprise, and industry can achieve in a few decades. Haifa is also a dramatic presentation of many diverse elements in the population working together for general progress and development.

Picture the enthusiasm of a group of far-seeing Jewish pioneers as they gaze over the sea from a promontory on Mt. Carmel on a spring morning forty years ago.

"A couple of breakwaters and quays and a little dredging would make Haifa a great port," suggests an engineer.

One member of the party looks over the barren swampy stretch of land that lay between Haifa and Acre, a bit in doubt until a bold, constructive idea comes to him.

"Those swamps could be drained. That flat area would be ideal for factories and workshops. There is plenty of vacant land for the erection of workers' settlements—simple inexpensive homes."

"Why should Haifa residents live close to the water's edge and swelter in the moist heat of summer?" asks another in the group, as he looks at the bare mountainside rising immediately behind the huddle of houses that constituted the town of that day.

"We could select a spot halfway up as the center of a new suburb and expand in both directions. We could erect hotels and sanitoriums atop Mt. Carmel and make it a wonderful vacation and health resort."

Their vision on that bright spring morning has come true. The development has progressed further than their fondest dreams. Already Haifa has a population of over 150,000, a particularly young and enterprising population. These young people came to work, to create something that they and countless others could enjoy.

Today Haifa is a clean, modern city, with tier on tier of white stone houses rising up the mountainside. Splendid asphalt highways make motoring a pleasure. At every turn in the road and atop the Carmel ridge, you glimpse wild ravines and romantic glades. The combination of a dazzling white city, the curve of the

sandy shore of Haifa Bay, and the sparkling blue of the Mediterranean Sea, gives Haifa a high rating among the scenic spots of the
world.

Theodor Herzl, the great leader of modern Zionism, declared
with remarkable foresight, at the first Congress of the World
Zionist Organization, meeting in Basle, Switzerland, in 1897:

"I believe that a wondrous generation of Jews will spring into
existence. . . . The Jews who wish will have their state. We shall
live at last as free men on our own soil, and die peacefully in our
own homes. The world will be freed by our liberty, enriched by
our wealth, magnified by our greatness. And whatever we attempt
there to accomplish for our own welfare, will react powerfully and
beneficently for the good of humanity."

CHAPTER TWO

So Small and Yet so Varied

⎍⎍⎍⎍⎍⎍⎍⎍⎍⎍⎍⎍⎍⎍⎍⎍

THE NEW life springing up in the once derelict Land of Israel has an exciting, dramatic quality that is felt by the visitor as well as by the participants in the rebirth of the country. Many of the Jews who have returned to their ancient homeland feel themselves to be instruments in some dimly outlined cosmic plan, as foretold by the Prophets of the Bible.

Ancient maps and an old legend place the Land of Israel as the center of the world, with Jerusalem the center of the Holy Land. Here, in a hundred-mile radius, in an area no bigger than Maryland or Vermont, is found a cross-section of peoples, religions, ways of living, and—most remarkable of all—samples of geographical features, climates, and soils.

The narrow coastal plain is bordered on the east with gently sloping hills, interspersed with mountains whose peaks rise occasionally to heights of 3,000 and 4,000 feet.

Farther to the east, the ground falls away rapidly to below sea level, and then rises abruptly to form the Mountains of Moab in Jordan. This unique gigantic cleft between the two mountain ranges—Israel's "Grand Canyon"—is the greatest rift in the earth's surface, sinking down at its lowest point 2600 feet toward the core of the planet!

At the bottom of this gorge, at various levels, lie three lakes— Lake Huleh, the Sea of Galilee, and the Dead Sea—connected by a swiftly flowing stream, the famous River Jordan. Here also was found a large papyrus swamp, a valley of tropical heat and fertility, and stretches of weirdly arid desolation.

The southern half of the Land of Israel, the Negev, was once little more than a great sandy waste. Recently it has become dotted with small Jewish settlements. It dips down, at the apex of an inverted triangle, to touch the waters of the Red Sea, close to the town of Elat. The monotony of huge sweeps of sand is broken by occasional rocky hills or escarpments, by cliffs and ravines in the Elat district, and by patches of green fields planted hopefully by young pioneers with the aid of piped water. Newcomers to Beersheba are adding another chapter to the long history of this town of seven wells.

Bright sunshine pervades the whole land, not only during the six rainless months from May to October, but also for much of the time during the remainder of the year. The sunshine glares on the sand-dunes and bare hillsides but smiles happily on rows of cabbages and cauliflowers, on orchards and vineyards, and on the purple bougainvillea climbing up little white houses. The old inhabitant protects himself from the glare by wrapping his long cloak about him. The new settler welcomes the sun by wearing shirts and shorts and by frequenting the beach in leisure hours.

When the rain comes, it pours down for a day or two, sometimes for three or four, and then for long intervals cloudless skies appear again. Not enough rainfall in the southern half of the country means serious drought. Good timing of the "first rains" and the "latter rains" means full ears of corn. An extra shower late in the Spring is called "golden rain," for it promises bumper harvests.

With the long dry season, there is no need to bother about umbrellas and galoshes for six whole months, and no danger of showers interfering with football games, picnics, garden parties, or vacation trips.

On the coastal plain—where most of the cities and towns are located, the weather during the winter months is mild and balmy, with temperatures near 50° F. Summer temperatures hover between 85° and 90°, with quite a bit of humidity.

The hill sections afford an almost perfect climate as the air is dry during the hot weather and fresh breezes from the sea arrive at nightfall. Most winter days are sparklingly clear and invigorating, with the mercury seldom falling below 40° F. A light blanket of snow coats the mountaintops only at rare intervals. A whole generation of children may grow up without having seen snow or frost.

The valleys lying below sea level take on a tropical character, providing a warm climate in the winter and becoming uncomfortably hot during the summer.

Israel's most trying weather condition is caused by the *khamsins.* These are hot winds from the eastern deserts that blow across the country for several days at a time during the spring and autumn months. The gentle breezes hold the warmth that might come from an open furnace door. Occasionally the winds have sucked up tiny particles of sand in passage over the deserts, and then when a khamsin arrives, a gray film obscures the sun, and windows and doors had better be tightly closed to keep out the fine dust. Naturally, such heat has an enervating, depressing effect. If the heat continues for a week, tempers become frayed, and the main topic of conversation is "How long will this khamsin last?" A sudden shift of the wind finally comes, and man and beast take a new lease on life.

These patterns of geography and weather are fairly typical of other countries bordering the Mediterranean and of many sections of the Middle East and western Asia, where millions of people are undernourished and poverty-stricken. Forty years ago, Palestine was no exception to the general situation described by Major C. S. Jarvis, former Governor of Sinai, which adjoins Israel to the south.

"In any Arab country," he wrote in his "Three Deserts," "one is faced by what one may call complete stagnation and lack of all effort. There are no roads, no cultivation worth speaking of, and no signs of progress or betterment of conditions. And yet all around one sees the ruins of a past civilization and prosperity; the fallen orchard and garden walls, ruined stone houses, and broken water channels."

Mark Twain, after visiting Palestine, called it "a hopeless, dreary, heartbroken land."

What has happened is that all parts of the population, natives as well as newcomers, have joined in a countrywide clean-up campaign and have given the land a face-lifting operation by cultivating many thousands of additional acres. The new settlers, bringing with them the gifts of Western civilization, came not to exploit the resources of the country and its inhabitants for stock-holders in a distant land, but to find security for themselves and their children, to create a new and better way of life.

In retrospect, it all seems simple and logical: drain the swamps, remove the sand-dunes encroaching on good soil along the coastal plain, fertilize the barren ground, dig wells, rebuild the hillside terraces, plant trees, improve the breeds of livestock and poultry. Construct hospitals and clinics and schools. Let public health nurses show people how to keep well, and have agricultural experts advise farmers how to grow good crops. Build ports and towns and cities. Install drainage systems. Provide a good water supply. Develop industries.

These are but a few of the first steps in the bringing of new life to the ancient land. They are so obviously necessary that they are remarkable only because the countries to the north, east, and south have not done likewise. Iraq has received untold millions in oil royalties, yet her farm workers are in the same undernour-ished, illiterate condition as they were fifty years ago, and her once fertile cornfields are still bare. Jordan, though originally part of the Palestine that the Jews hoped to redeem, was separated by the British in 1922 and has remained a sparsely inhabited land, far removed from twentieth-century ideas under Arab rule. The great majority of Egypt's toiling millions live in miserable hovels and are weakened by disease.

Water supply sets a limit to human activity, so it was fortunate that among the pioneers who came to Palestine from eastern Europe twenty-five years ago was a noted engineer who utilized the rapid descent of the Jordan River to generate electricity—for with electric power, pumps could bring water from deep underground limestone formations where winter rains are stored.

The Jordan rises amid the melting snows of nine-thousand-foot Mt. Hermon in Lebanon and empties into the Dead Sea below sea level. Its upper reaches flow into Lake Huleh, and from there the river cuts its way south to the Sea of Galilee. In the nine miles between the two lakes, the river falls nine hundred feet in small cascades and rapids. From the southern end of the Sea of Galilee, the Jordan continues to descend through many twists and turns and whirlpools until it reaches the Dead Sea, whose surface is 1300 feet below sea level and whose floor is 1300 feet farther down!

A new water network will link together all the country's water resources, including rivers, springs, and thousands of artesian wells. An immense water storage dam is being constructed in the Natufa Valley, completely surrounded by hills, midway between the Sea of Galilee and the Mediterranean. When completed, Lake Natufa will hold 26 billion gallons of water. A dike will divide the lake into equal halves. It is planned to triple the area of irrigated land, and so vastly increase crop production. The surplus waters of the north will be piped to the parched Negev and make possible the cultivation of a million acres in this present desert wasteland as well as the extension of the cultivated areas on the borders of the Jordan.

Experts report that there are plenty of hydro-electric possibilities with which to develop a Jordan Valley Authority on lines so successfully carried out by the Tennessee Valley Authority in the U.S.A. While awaiting the consent of bordering Arab nations for such projects, Israel has increased its electric production in other power stations. Industrial use of electricity has tripled.

The temperate climate of the hills, the warmer weather of the plains, and the torrid heat in the valleys lying below sea level facilitate the growing of a remarkable variety of fruits and vegetables the year round.

In the United States, we get oranges and grapefruit from Florida and California, apples from Oregon and Washington, potatoes from Maine and Idaho, bananas from Brazil, dates from Iraq, and olives from Spain. Israel produces all of them within its 7,800 square miles!

Oranges, grapefruit, tangerines, and lemons thrive so well in the sandy soil of the coastal plain and in the valleys that Israel has already become the second largest citrus exporting country in the world. Mile after mile of neat orange groves help to give the land a well-cared-for look, and now the sweet scent of orange blossoms has replaced the acrid odor of dunghills, once so characteristic of Arab villages.

Interspersed between orange groves, dairy farms, and poultry runs are patches of intense color. Side by side grow long rows of flaming gladiolus, long-stemmed roses, snapdragons, blue corn-flowers, larkspur, delphinium, linaria, freesia, dahlias, zinnias, and all shades of sweet-peas. Gathered in the early morning hours by skilful fingers, they are shipped by motor car and appear the same day in the flower shops of Tel Aviv, Haifa, and Jerusalem, where they are eagerly purchased for home decoration.

The plain of Esdraelon, known as the *Emek* (the Valley), starts a little southeast of Haifa and extends eastwards to the vicinity of Beisan in the Jordan Valley. In ancient days, caravans from Baghdad and Damascus and other ancient cities to the east, bearing spices and silks and choice rugs, as well as sacks of grain, passed through this great highway to reach the coastal plain on their way to Egypt. This is Israel's most spectacular exhibit of the change-over from swampland to food-producing area, for every acre has been carefully cultivated by young men and women working in small units. Here are grown wheat and barley, sesame and fodder crops, all kinds of vegetables, and grapefruit. Though the soil is fertile, it is difficult to work with, for it becomes heavy mud when it rains and hard clay in dry weather.

The Huleh Plain, extending from the foothills of the Lebanon to Rosh Pinah, a distance of twenty miles, is like a green carpet surrounded on three sides by hills and mountains. Here fruit trees and vineyards have been planted in addition to vegetables and fodder crops. In the center of the plain was once the 15,000-acre papyrus swamp, one of the most northern of its kind in the world. Beneath the swamp, to a depth of twenty and thirty feet, lay a rich, black humus—a solid mine of fructifying soil. Engineers have drained the swamp and have plans to apply layers of this rich earth to the neighboring arid mountainsides.

Lake Huleh is small and intimate, like an Alpine crystal pool. Here young Jewish pioneers have established modern settlements devoted to fishing and farming. White pelicans and storks in large numbers visit this region in their overland flights, and occasionally kingfishers with black and white tips and falcons with far-spreading wings may be seen.

On the hilly slopes of Israel are found most of the olive trees, which seem to fit naturally into the landscape, and indeed they have been at home here since time immemorial. Many of the trees are centuries old—some dating back to Roman and Crusader times—and their fantastically gnarled and twisted trunks show evidence of their great age. Their silver-green leaves shimmer in the sunshine the entire year.

On hillside terraces are thousands of fig trees, whose green and purple fruit is particularly luscious when eaten immediately after picking. Here also are apricots—called for some reason *mish-mish,* and almonds, whose delicate pink and white blossoms make miniature fairylands out of some otherwise bleak background. The pomegranate and the carob are old-timers in the Holy Land, but other fruits now keep them company. Plums and peaches, apples and pears, and even cherries are grown with success. Why not—

with sunshine, water, good soil, the right kind of climate, and good care?

In the Jordan Valley, where temperatures soar to 110° F. in summer, date palms and banana plantations bask in sunshine. Many other tropical and semi-tropical fruits thrive here, such as avocado pears, guavas, mangoes, loquats, anonas, and papayas. Here four crops of vegetables are grown each year and a constant succession of varied blooms keeps the flower farms a mass of color. Grapes grow well in many sections. As the time of ripening varies with the location of the vineyards, the grape season lasts for several months—a real joy, as the grapes are particularly delicious.

The supply of vegetables has grown by leaps and bounds, spurred by the high prices received for them. Tomatoes, onions and garlic, cucumbers, cauliflower, eggplant, cabbage, and potatoes are the leading varieties. It seems as if every vegetable that grows in other countries, from the lowly carrot and parsnip to the more aristocratic asparagus and celery, does well in Israel. Squash and pumpkins develop to great size; artichokes, turnips, kohlrabi and broccoli are very plentiful. Most of the population seems to have enlarged its diet of beans and lentils to include lettuce, spinach, beets, and radishes.

If you think that gently sloping hills and valleys in Israel look fairly similar to those in New Jersey or Pennsylvania, you will be quite wrong. Despite the recent planting of fifteen million saplings, forested hills are the exception rather than the rule. There are no grassy fields and very few winding streams. No comfortable looking farmhouses and red barns. Absence of trees means lack of lumber, so houses are made of baked mud or concrete in the plains and of stone or concrete in the hills. Walls of carefully piled loose stones or cactus hedges separate one man's field from his neighbor's and line the roads. There are no advertising billboards for these have never been allowed to disturb the quiet charm of the countryside.

To prevent heavy winter rains from washing the soil down the slopes, the good farmer in ancient days built low walls of the rocks and stones which, fortunately, were near at hand. Soil was filled in against the walls, the upper surface forming level strips of land on which trees were planted and crops raised. These terraces, when built up the side of a hill, resemble steps a giant might climb with seven-league boots. They are often only a few yards wide, and the farmer must lead his horse or camel carefully when turning corners at his plowing. When kept in good repair, the terrace walls last for centuries and prevent erosion.

But for generations the inhabitants of Palestine were heedless of broken terrace walls. Trees were cut down time after time by invading armies. Goats were allowed to nibble away at young shoots and saplings. With no walls or trees to hold the soil, the rains have swept the red top soil into deep gullies, carried it down to the plains and out to sea, and now in many places only great rocks, which were once two and three feet below the surface, may be seen. The mountainsides seem to be sprouting stones. The Arabs have a legend that when God made the world, He put all the stones which were to cover it into two bags and gave them to an angel, and while the angel was flying over Palestine, one bag broke! A beginning has been made in the repair of terrace walls and re-foresting the hills, but it is a slow and painstaking job.

Redeeming the soil goes forward acre by acre, terrace by terrace, and is the work of individuals or small groups, urged by their own initiative. Here are no large food corporations with thousands of employees and immense capital. Even on the fertile coastal plain, holdings are small. Herds of cattle and flocks of sheep are merely sample editions of the livestock that browse on the western prairies of the United States or on the great plains of Australia.

What sort of mineral deposits are found in Israel? Plenty of limestone, marble, basalt, and gypsum for building purposes; shale, lime, and the right kind of sands for cement and glass-making; asphalt and bituminous limestone for road construction; salt that can be used without refining; sulphur and phosphates. There is a great possibility that oil will be found, but it has not yet been discovered. Iron, copper, and manganese deposits exist, and plans are being made for the industrial exploitation of these valuable assets.

Palestine's chief mineral wealth is the supply of chemicals found in the waters of the Dead Sea. Here was a vast treasure trove of half a dozen chemicals that the world needs—awaiting the magic wand of a skilful engineer to make them available for use.

The Dead Sea, or "Salt Sea" as it was sometimes called, is a geographical wonder. It receives six million tons of water daily from the Jordan River and five small streams in Jordan, but it has no exit for the water except by evaporation. The streams which feed the Dead Sea are unusually salty, and when the hot sun evaporates the moisture, the salts and minerals remain, making the remaining water five times as salty as ocean water.

A large plant of the Dead Sea Works, Ltd., the holder of the concession for extracting the chemicals, is located at the southern end of the sea, which is forty-eight miles long and has an average width of ten miles. Evaporation is speeded up for commercial purposes by drawing off the water into shallow pans covering thousands of acres on the flat shores and, after the brine is concentrated by the action of the sun and wind, it is dug out and sent to the chemical plants in little railway cars that run on special sidings. Convoys of trucks carry thousands of tons of potash, bromine, potassium, calcium and table salt on a new road linking Sdom at the Southern end to Beersheba and then on to the coast for local use and shipment abroad. It is estimated that billions of tons of minerals may eventually be extracted.

Beaches, mountains, and lakes lend themselves to all kinds of vacation plans and outdoor sports. Boy and girl scouts and adult walking parties have no trouble in finding interesting goals for short hikes or overnight camping trips. Besides the natural scenery, there are hundreds of places to visit associated with history or legend.

The camel trail still runs close to the site near Nablus where Joseph's brethren threw him into a pit and later sold him to passing merchants on their way to Egypt. They still make coats of many colors in that district and pits are dug in the fields for lime-stone burning. The exploits of Samson may be visualized in the Vale of Sorek, where Delilah had her home. Rachel's Tomb lies close to the roadside between Jerusalem and Bethlehem; and the Cave of Machpelah, which Abraham bought from the Hittite for a family burial place, is a shrine in Hebron.

Excellent bathing beaches line the coast, and those living inland are not too far away to make use of them on weekends and holi-days. Bat Yam, south of Tel Aviv, and Naharia, north of Haifa, are typical of the small seaside towns which have sprung up in recent years. Modern white concrete homes are surrounded with flower gardens, and incomes are supplemented by renting out rooms to vacationists. A few of the houses are labeled hotels or pensions, but they do not vary much in appearance from their neighbors. The installation of electric light and modern bath-rooms is taken as a matter of course.

Nathania, a rapidly growing town between Tel Aviv and Haifa, has a beach-front edged with buff-colored limestone cliffs. The cliffs, in combination with the intense blue of the Mediterranean and the glistening green of miles of orange groves, have led to this region being called the Israel Riviera.

Safed is an ancient mountain town where time until recent days stood still. Its quaint bazaars, winding stepped streets, and old synagogues have changed very little since the time when this spot became famous for its Rabbinical schools and the study of the mystical teachings of the Kabbala. It had a printing press as early as 1563.

Hanita, one of the new settlements near the northern boundary of Israel, is a small cluster of white houses, surrounded by color-ful gardens and rock terraces, with a glorious view of the shining sea to the west. A well has been drilled which provides abundant water. Hundreds of acres of barren hillside have been cleared of boulders and planted with apple and pear trees. Wheat and barley and vegetables are harvested in the valley close by. Fresh milk and cream, cheese and butter are provided by fifty cows. Five

thousand chickens are laying eggs, and bees in two hundred hives
are busy making honey. A great deal of courage and hard work
lie behind the achievements of this little group of 150 young settlers who have fashioned a small paradise out of a rocky mountain
top.

Israel possesses unique winter resorts in that strange tropical
valley lying below the usual surface of the earth. Its spectacular
scenery vies with that of Arizona and New Mexico. Local residents already take advantage of these resorts and once they have
been discovered by foreign visitors, it is probable that they may
become international spas.

In December or January in times of peace, when transit over
boundaries is facilitated, you may leave Jerusalem shivering in
chilly blasts of cold rain and descend in less than an hour to the
warmth of a balmy summer's day. You may take a dip in the
buoyant waters of the Dead Sea which are said to possess curative
powers. After that, perhaps you will have afternoon tea while you
watch the soft afterglow of the setting sun turn the mysterious
barren mountains into an enchanting background of kaleidoscopic
color.

Along the eastern shore of the Dead Sea rise the Mountains of
Moab, three thousand feet high. The tawny limestone cliffs,
capped with softer chalk and streaked with black basalt, are re-
flected in the still waters below. The high peak of Pisgah on Mt.
Nebo, from which Moses viewed the Promised Land, can be seen
in a line with the north shore.

Near the first deep valley on the east shore are the Hot Springs
of Kallirhoe, famous in Roman times. Here you can bathe in
natural pools of warm sulphurous water. Some miles to the north
of the Springs are the vividly colored gorges of the Wadi Zerka
and farther south are the ruins of the Herodian Castle of Machæ-
rus, where John the Baptist was beheaded and where Salome
danced.

About halfway down the length of the Dead Sea is the mouth
of the River Arnon. During the dry season it is possible to walk

up the riverbed for several miles, while gigantic cliffs tower on either side, as far as a high waterfall.

At the southwestern end of the Sea is Jebel Usdum, a vast mountain of pure rock salt. High up on the cliff, a dozen Arabs may be seen quarrying the salt by chopping off chunks from the mountainside. In this section, a pillar of salt in human form is still known as Lot's wife, the one who looked back at the burning cities of Sodom and Gomorrah, in the Biblical story.

One of the loveliest oases in the world and a town that has had a continuous history for eight thousand years is Jericho, which you can visit on your way from Jerusalem to the Dead Sea. The modern mud-brick village, surrounded by date palms, orange groves, and banana plantations, is a mile away from the ruined walls of the old Canaanitish city which Joshua took so many centuries ago. You can easily imagine why King Herod made this fertile spot his winter residence and that its revenue from dates and balsam were once so great that Mark Antony gave the town as a present to Cleopatra. Close by are the ancient pools to which still come sheep and cattle in old, picturesque style, accompanied by shepherds and herdsmen. The lush green of Jericho is heightened by the desolate wilderness roundabout. Not far off is the barren Mount of Temptation, where Jesus is reputed to have spent forty days resisting the lure of ambition. The old Greek monastery, clinging to the steep side of the mountain, is still inhabited by friendly monks.

The ancient town of Tiberias, on the shores of the sparkling Sea of Galilee, or Lake Tiberias, retains an oriental atmosphere in some of its narrow streets and along the quayside. However, its beautiful homes, hotels, and school buildings in the newer sections of the town, rising on the hillsides, are very modern. A lakeshore drive leads to the Tiberias Hot Springs Pavilions, where thousands of men and women bathe daily in the medicinal waters during the winter months, seeking a cure for their rheumatism, arthritis, or other ailments.

The Sea of Galilee, or Lake Tiberias, nearly thirteen miles long and eight miles wide at its broadest expanse, has a rich supply of fish, and young Jewish fishermen from the lake-side settlements of Ginosar, Ein Geb, Degania, and Kinneret have eagerly welcomed the task of laying nets and bringing in the catches. Rowboats and motor launches are available for visitors.

At the northern end of the lake is Capernaum, where remarkably well-preserved ruins of an imposing synagogue from Roman times may be seen. It was to this place that Jesus came after leaving Nazareth. Here he gathered his disciples, and went out with them to the villages which dotted this region in his day. From Peter's boat, Jesus performed the miracle of the draught of the fishes. It was the Sea of Galilee that was referred to in the words: "Jesus went unto them, walking on the sea."

Israel is not only a blend of past and present, it is a land of challenge. It keeps its secrets and its treasures for those who listen and understand its voices. Sun, water, and soil have now joined with man to bring once again health, prosperity, and beauty.

Walter Clay Lowdermilk, a soil expert of the U.S. Department of Agriculture, after a tour of inspection in 1939, declared:

"Along with the record of decay in the Holy Land, we found a thoroughgoing effort to restore the ancient fertility of the long-neglected soil. This effort is the most remarkable we have seen while studying land use in twenty-four countries. It is being made by Jewish settlers who fled to Palestine from the hatreds and persecutions of Europe. . . . They are doing something there that has significance for the whole Near East and the whole world."

CHAPTER THREE

"A Thousand Years Are But as Yesterday"

⎍⎍⎍⎍⎍⎍⎍⎍⎍⎍⎍⎍⎍⎍⎍⎍

HISTORY in the Land of Israel stretches all the way back to the days of the cave dwellers. This small area, as the scene of man's gradual development, the meeting place of East and West, highlights the perpetual search for food, trade routes, and power. The known area of the Earth has expanded in ever-widening circles until now all of it is included in our "one world," but the Land of Israel still remains the center. No wonder that each occurrence in the Holy Land seems to send out a ripple that reaches to the farthest circumference!

Skeleton remains found in caves near Mt. Carmel and the Sea of Galilee, and an elephant's tusk measuring six feet long, dug up from the bed of the River Jordan, date back, say the scholars, more than 50,000 years. In caves near the Sea of Galilee, archæologists have discovered flint axes which were used by men to till the soil 100,000 years ago.

About 10,000 years ago, man found out that it wasn't necessary to remain in caves. He could build a hut or a house. Jericho, Megiddo, Beisan and Lachish are among the ancient sites in Palestine that were occupied by town-dwellers many thousands of years ago. As time went on, houses were built with spacious central courtyards. Later on came palaces, fortified walls and towers, temples, synagogues, churches, monasteries, and mosques, and today apartment houses, office buildings, and police posts.

31

The clays found in many parts of Israel were used in pottery-making in the dim past, when newcomers who had mastered the art of ceramics invaded the land. Previously, stone had been the only material used. Other settlers introduced copper, bronze, and iron; still others gold and silver. Today's immigrants have brought tin, aluminum, steel, and plastics.

Early man in the Land of Israel knew only sheep and goats as domestic animals, but when the camel and horse and donkey were introduced, he found many uses for them. In fact, they made as great a change in his life as the automobile and the airplane have made to man in the present era.

Wheat and barley were developed into valuable food plants by the first farmers, and the finding of samples of wild wheat in this neighborhood has given rise to the belief that the "staff of life" may have had its origin here. The olive tree also grew wild at first. Figs, grapes, and dates were other early sources of food. Also apricots and pomegranates, and almonds, walnuts, and pistachio nuts.

Records of events, using the Hebrew alphabet then current, were made in Israel about thirty centuries ago. It is interesting to note that many of the letters of the English alphabet have been indirectly derived from the Hebrew. The ancient Greeks learned about the Hebrew letters when trading along the shores of the eastern Mediterranean. The first two letters of the Hebrew alphabet are "aleph" and "bet," and the first two letters of the Greek alphabet are "alpha" and "beta." The Romans, in turn, borrowed from the Greek for their Latin, and Latin provided the basis for the English and many other western alphabets. The Cuneiform writing of the Sumerians, who lived in Mesopotamia, and the Heiroglyphic writing of the Egyptians preceded the first known Hebrew records.

Palestine was well placed geographically to receive new ideas, as it lay between two centers of ancient civilization—Mesopotamia (now modern Iraq) and Egypt. The peoples of these two centers exchanged products, and their caravans passed through the land along inland or coastal routes. Sometimes the traders of Palestine acted as middlemen or expediters.

Through thousands of years, the inhabitants of these two territories made periodic attempts to enlarge their dominions; and the control of the bridge between them—Palestine—passed from one to the other as events dictated the rise and fall of each to power. The peoples living in Mesopotamia, across the desert to the east of Palestine, were known by a somewhat confusing variety of names as first one and then another group obtained supremacy. Here lived the Sumerians, the Hittites, the Assyrians, the Arameans, the Babylonians, the Persians, and farther to the east, the Mongols.

Population pressures, droughts, and famines also brought many people to the fertile hills and plains of Palestine. Among these in the dim past were the Semites from the interior deserts of Arabia. A little more than thirty centuries ago, the Philistines and the Phœnicians, known as the "Peoples of the Seas," came as refugees to the shores of the eastern Mediterranean from the region around the Aegean Sea and gave the name of Philistia to the Land of Canaan—from which the name Palestine is derived.

The Greeks, under Alexander the Great, were the first of the great western powers to expand to the east on the road to world conquest. Palestine came under the Greek sphere of influence after Alexander captured Tyre in 332 B.C. The Greeks were supplanted by the Romans three hundred years later when Pompey took Jerusalem. After the Roman Empire was split up, Palestine lay within the territory of the Byzantine emperors, who ruled from Constantinople.

Next the Arabs, inspired by Mohammed, gained ascendency in world affairs, overrunning Palestine in 636 A.D., before extending their sway to Northern Africa and Spain. During the 11th and 12th centuries, Europeans, coming to Palestine as Crusaders, founded the Latin Kingdom of Jerusalem. They were ousted by Saladin and the Mamelukes from Egypt.

Again and again invading armies brought slaughter and destruction. Inhabitants were slain by the sword, and towns and cities sacked and set on fire. Great forests were cut down, and during periods of insecurity the farmers had difficulty in raising crops. But the greatest devastation occurred when the conquering hordes of the Mongols or Huns, sweeping down from Asia in the 13th century, subjugated Palestine and all the neighboring countries, in an era when their sway extended from China to East Prussia. They were noted for bringing massacre and ruin to every country they visited.

After the power of the Mongols waned, the Turks in the 16th century supplanted both Arabs and Mongols. And finally,—in the 20th century,—in 1917, British and Australian troops, aided by French, Indian, New Zealand, and Jewish Battalions, occupied Palestine in the course of World War I. It remained in the British sphere of influence, under a Mandate from the League of Nations, until the United Nations Assembly, in an historic decision on November 29, 1947, called for the creation of Jewish and Arab independent states. The State of Israel came into existence on May 14, 1948.

When you go to Israel today, you may easily visit hundreds of historical sites and holy places and gain a better understanding of the peoples of ancient times and the conditions under which they lived.

Fifty years ago it would have been quite a different matter. There were then no good roads and no hotels. It was unsafe to travel in many parts of the country. Sanitary conditions were distinctly bad. Very little was known about many of the ancient sites. Investigations were not encouraged, and layers of sand and debris covered the ruins.

It was only a hundred years ago that scientists from America, England, Germany, and France began to survey and map out the land and search for the places mentioned in the Bible and made famous by great events of history. Often they came singly. Few stayed the year round. Funds gave out. Cholera stopped their work. Still, they were persistent and finally produced maps and many volumes of information. In 1848 an American expedition explored the Dead Sea and the Jordan River. In 1865 a few friends met in London and established the Palestine Exploration Fund, and this made possible a survey west of the Jordan.

But the science of modern archæology had yet to be born. It was only in 1883 that Sir Flinders Petrie, called the father of modern archæology, came to the conclusion that the glaze or the shape or the design of pottery changed rapidly and clearly from time to time. He and other archæologists were later able to say that this and this sort of glaze was used in 500 B.C., and that and that fashion became the style in 220 A.D. Formerly nothing had a meaning unless it was an inscription, a coin, or a piece of sculpture.

Now archæologists—in their great treasure-hunts—search for pieces of pottery, flint, jewelry, tools, and weapons. They are able to tell at a glance the kind of people who lived at a certain place and when they lived there, from these small objects which have lain buried for centuries and sometimes for millenniums.

Clay utensils were not of great value, so when people migrated or fled or were killed on the spot, no attention was paid to pieces of pottery lying around. There they remained. Of course, most objects became broken, so that now when archæologists find small fragments of pottery—called sherds—the first job is to piece them together, often very much like a jigsaw puzzle. When some pieces are missing in a jar, jug, lamp, or bowl, as the case may be, the empty space is filled in with a little plaster.

Sir Flinders came to Palestine in 1890 to search for the site of ancient Lachish. He went to a place called Umm Lakis and looked for old sherds or other remains. None could be found. Then he noticed a mound in the vicinity, called Tell el-Hesy. He found on top of the hillock, almost on the surface, articles dating back to the Greek era of 450 B.C. He and his workers dug deeper, and as they went farther down, they came across mementos of earlier and still earlier times. Twenty feet down, they discovered ruins of the Phœnicians, who must have occupied the site about 900 B.C.

At forty-five feet, ruins dated back to 1400 B.C. Nothing but plain earth was found below this level.

Sir Flinders made these deductions: The first people who lived here were killed in some raid or battle, or were driven into exile. New people came along afterwards and built homes on the ruins which they found. Then they too, or their children or grandchildren, were driven away, or an earthquake may have killed them. Sand and dirt covered the town until once again new settlers reoccupied the site. Eventually, the newcomers settled on an adjacent piece of land.

As the contending armies came and went, many places were built up, destroyed, and built again, and each time the level of the site was slightly raised as new foundations were built on the ruins of the old.

There are innumerable hillocks scattered throughout Israel and Jordan, and many of them, particularly those hills with flat tops are "tells"—ancient sites where people have lived in the past. Bits of a wall, an archway, or a door or a cistern—but most of all the sherds and other objects of everyday use, tell the date of each level of settlement.

Jericho's excavators followed the town's history stage by stage from the invasion of Joshua back to the days of Abraham and Lot, and then back still farther, paring off layer after layer of the town's ancient dust until—seventeen layers below the 2000 B.C. level—they reached down to the days of 6000 B.C. The ten lowest layers marked what is called the neolithic age. Even then Jericho was a settled urban center, the market town for the surrounding pastoral and agricultural communities.

The whole sweep of the centuries has been revivified by the archæologists at Bethshan, a "tell" close to the modern town of Beisan. Here, on the ancient highroad between Damascus and Egypt, excavations show strata, one above the other, which represent the city under Philistine, Israelite, Assyrian, Babylonian, and Persian rule. The upper layers are from the Greek, Roman, Byzantine, and Arab periods until the present day. The same

Beisan which was the goal of Allenby's cavalry in September 1918, had seen Saul and Judas Maccabeus, Pompey and his Roman legions, Cleopatra, Vespasian, Richard the Lion-Hearted, Saladin, and Napoleon.

Since the pioneering days of the making of maps, surveys, and geographical and historical atlases, the American School of Oriental Research has been established in Jerusalem. A government department of Antiquities has been in operation, and the Hebrew University, the British School of Archæology, and various scientific societies have all devoted much effort to illuminating Palestine's long history. More information has been uncovered in the last few decades than during the preceding thousand years.

Against the Palestine background, we get a new appreciation of periods of time, of the rise and fall of nations, and of the ebb and flow of culture and civilization and progress between East and West. We begin to realize what a new melting pot of nationalities the United States has been for the past century compared to the mixing of peoples that has been taking place in Palestine during fifty centuries.

Palestine was frequently considered Southern Syria. Often it was annexed to Egypt. From time to time it formed part of great empires. The only time that it became a distinct political and independent unit was during the era when the Jews or Hebrews governed the land.

The Children of Israel entered the Promised Land after their sojourn and slavery in Egypt. On their way there, they had a forty-year period of wandering in the Sinai Desert, during which they were being welded into nationhood under the leadership of Moses. The Ancient Hebrews preserved the tradition that their forefather Abraham had come to the Land of Canaan from a town in Mesopotamia—Ur of the Chaldees—and that this land was destined to belong to them and their descendants. We read in the Book of Genesis:

"Now the Lord had said unto Abram, Get thee out of
thy country, and out of thy birthplace, and from thy

father's house, unto the land that I will show thee. And
I will make of thee a great nation, and I will bless thee
and make thy name great; and thou shalt be a blessing."

During a period of two to three hundred years, the Twelve
Tribes extended their conquests over the groups they found occupying the Land of Canaan.

King David, about the year 1000 B.C.—three thousand years ago
—captured the stronghold of Jerusalem and made it the capital
of his kingdom. His rule extended over the Philistines on the
coast and over the Edomites, Moabites, and Ammonites to the
east of the Jordan. He established his authority in Damascus and
as far east as the Euphrates Valley. All this was possible because
of a lull in the rivalry between the Egyptians and the Assyrians.

His son, King Solomon, fortified the wall which surrounded
Jerusalem, erected the Temple as the spiritual center of the nation, and built a magnificent palace where he reigned in Oriental
splendor. Solomon developed the country's resources and encouraged trade and industry in the three to four hundred towns of
that day. The reservoirs that he constructed a few miles to the
south of Bethlehem are still called "Solomon's Pools." The quarries from which his workers hewed the marble for the Temple
walls lie close to the Damascus Gate of Jerusalem. The blast
furnaces used in his copper refining plant have been discovered
at the site of Ezion-Geber, his seaport on the Gulf of Aqaba.

"King Solomon made a fleet of ships in Ezion-Geber,
which is beside Elath on the shore of the Red Sea in the
land of Edom. Once in three years the fleet came in
bringing gold, silver, ivory, apes, peacocks, a very great
amount of sandalwood, and precious stones."—I Kings
ix:26; x:22.

For the next thousand years, until 70 A.D., the Jews remained
the leading factor in the Land of Israel, although their power and
numbers were diminished by internal strife and foreign domination.

The peace and prosperity of Solomon's era did not last long. Damascus and Edom revolted, and the Kingdom broke into two parts—Israel and Judah. Assyria resumed her aggression after several centuries of peace and annexed the northern Kingdom of Israel, exiling most of its inhabitants—sometimes called "The Lost Ten Tribes." After another century had gone by, the Babylonians, who had risen to power, conquered the southern Kingdom of Judah, destroyed the Temple in Jerusalem, and deported many leading citizens to Babylon. The Book of Esther records events that took place during this time of exile in Babylon.

Fifty years later, the Persians had supplanted the Babylonians as the leading power in Mesopotamia, and they permitted the Jews to return to their homeland, to rebuild their Temple, and to lay the foundations of a new commonwealth.

Egypt, Syria, and Greece imposed successive economic and political yokes which the Jews were able to throw off from time to time. The remarkable victory of this period, under the leadership of the Maccabees, is still celebrated during the festival of Chanukah. About 100 B.C., the Jewish state again held all the present territory of Israel, the cities of Jordan, and the southern parts of Syria.

However, the treaty of friendship which the Jews had made with the expanding Roman Empire did not deter the Roman general, Pompey, from taking Jerusalem in 63 B.C. Judea was made part of the Roman province of Syria, though the kings of Judea still enjoyed a great measure of independence. Herod the Great reigned from 37 B.C. to 4 A.D. After his death, Judea was controlled by Roman procurators, and it was during the rule of one of these, Pontius Pilate, that the events of the Gospels took place.

The first struggle for independence against Roman tyranny ended with the sacking of Jerusalem and the burning of the Temple by Titus in 70 A.D. The second and final revolt, under Bar Cochba, came to an end in 135 A.D., after three and a half years of fighting, in which half a million Jews were killed.

A hundred years previous, the country had been at the height of its prosperity, with a population, estimated conservatively, of three million. But now—for a hundred years—no Jew was permitted to live in Jerusalem. Tiberias became the new center of learning. The inhabitants of the land were dispersed to Babylon, to Egypt, to Arabia, and to Europe. Jews continued to live in the Land of Israel but they never regained a dominant position until our own days.

Some five hundred years later, the Jews of Tiberias put a force of 20,000 soldiers in the field as an aid to the Persians who were trying to oust the Byzantines, the successors to the Romans. But they fought on the losing side and a great massacre of Jews resulted in 628 A.D. Soon after, the days of Byzantine rule came to an end.

Mohammed and his successor, Caliph Abu-Bakr, had succeeded in uniting the Beduin tribes of Arabia, and they changed from raiding each other to attacking the Byzantines in Palestine and Syria. They finally won decisive victories; and from 636 A.D. onwards, Palestine became part of Syria under Arab domination. There was no great influx of Arabs, however, and the Caliphs ruled from Damascus, Baghdad, and Cairo through the years.

Islam made many converts by the sword in other lands, but in Palestine religious penetration was effected by more peaceful means. Those who embraced Islam were exempted from a tax which all "non-believers" had to pay. There were few Jewish converts, but gradually in the course of centuries most of the other inhabitants became Moslems and the Arabic language was put into general use.

Jews reëstablished a religious center in Jerusalem, and continued to live in a few other urban centers through more centuries of invasion, famine, and oppressive taxation. From time to time, Jewish immigration to Palestine gained headway. In the 13th century, three hundred rabbis from France settled in Jerusalem. Other refugees from European persecution arrived in Acre. The expulsion of the Jews from Spain and Portugal at the end of the

15th century led to an influx to Palestine. Jerusalem and Safed received most of these refugees, who possessed a high degree of culture. Another wave of immigration took place in the 18th century.

However, economic prospects were poor and there seemed very little opportunity to earn a living. Soon it was mainly the old and the pious who found their way to the Land of Israel to spend their last years on the sacred soil of their ancient homeland. Jewish communities throughout the world kept in touch with Palestine through traveling traders, scholars, and collectors of funds for the Jewish needy of Jerusalem.

Jerusalem had always remained the center of Jewish hopes and prayers. At the Seder service, ushering in the Passover festival of freedom, there is an unforgettable moment of wishful thinking, when everyone present exclaims:

"Next year in Jerusalem!"

During the two thousand years of their dispersal, the Jews had made a practice of reading the Bible, which renewed for them the details of their history and their traditions. No matter how far distant, they had kept the harvest festivals of the Land of Israel. They had prayed for the "first rains" and the "latter rains" which were so important to crops in Palestine. Their morning prayers had included the words:

"Oh bring us in peace from the four corners of the earth and make us go upright to our land."

In the latter part of the 19th century and the beginning of the 20th, this longing and love for the place that had been the scene of their former glory reached a new intensity, due primarily to the bitter persecution which the Jews suffered in many lands in Europe.

No matter if the "Land of Milk and Honey" had become a stretch of desolation. No matter if the Turkish officials did not welcome new settlers. Palestine meant home—the Land of Israel. That was enough. They decided to make their dream come true —and a new era began.

It was Theodor Herzl who brought the modern Zionist movement into the realm of practical politics, although there had been individuals and small groups previously who had worked for the resettlement of Jews on the soil of Palestine. In 1896, Herzl formulated his thesis in a small booklet, entitled "The Jewish State." A year later, he and his fellow-workers sent out a call for the First World Zionist Congress. This Congress declared:

"The aim of Zionism is to create for the Jewish people a publicly recognized, legally secured homeland in Palestine."

Until his death in 1904, Herzl devoted himself to bringing the Zionist cause to the attention of kings, rulers, and leading men in many lands, but without much success. People were indifferent and his ideas were often thought impractical by the wealthy. It was the faith, the hard work, and the collection of small sums by the Jewish masses that provided the impetus toward the return to Zion in the early years of the movement.

Plans were carefully drawn up for reclaiming the ancient heritage. Every foot of ground was to be bought and paid for. There was to be no exploitation of labor, either among Jew or non-Jew. A Jewish National Fund (Keren Kayemet) was established in 1901, to be used for the purchase of land in Palestine, to be held in trust for the whole people. This land could be leased but not sold. This land must be worked by the lessee and his family. A general colonizing fund, known as the Palestine Foundation Fund (Keren Hayesod), assisted new settlers with housing, equipment, tools, livestock, and training.

The world was groping to find solutions to problems of land ownership, fair distribution of wealth, improvement of working conditions for employees. The young idealists who left their books and work-benches in the lands of eastern Europe for work on the soil in the Land of Israel were determined to find the answers through bold experiments. They were mindful of the words of the Prophet Amos:

"And I will turn the captivity of My people Israel, and
they shall build the waste cities, and inhabit them; and

they shall plant vineyards and drink the wine thereof;
they shall also make gardens and eat the fruit of them."

In 1917, Great Britain took the lead in publicly backing the Zionist Movement in the Balfour Declaration, which stated: "His Majesty's Government view with favor the establishment in Palestine of a National Home for the Jewish People, and will use their best endeavors to facilitate the achievement of this object, it being clearly understood that nothing shall be done which may prejudice the civil and religious rights of existing non-Jewish communities in Palestine, or the rights and political status enjoyed by the Jews in any other country."

The Mandate to administer Palestine, given to Great Britain by the League of Nations after World War I and the breakup of the Turkish Empire, incorporated this declaration as a sort of charter, and it was confirmed and approved by the United States and fifty-two other nations.

The next thirty years constituted an important transition period. Many of the British officials and administrators who came to Palestine had had experience in various parts of the British Empire, and they brought this knowledge to the many problems of the Holy Land. Laws had to be redrafted and courts set up. A police force had to be organized. A system of land settlement was worked out, and instruction given in modern agricultural methods. Government Departments of Health and Education were established.

Despite many unexpected difficulties in addition to those that had been foreseen, in the short span of less than half a century 700,000 Jews became permanent settlers in Palestine, with modern Hebrew as their language, with a unifying spirit and a creative culture. Side by side with the removal of the stones from the fields, had come the establishment of a great Hebrew University on Mt. Scopus.

During World War II, Palestine constituted an Allied stronghold that could be relied on in the fight against Hitler. Thirty thousand Jews had volunteered for service in the British army, navy, and airforce, had become members of commando units, suicide squads, the Jewish Brigade, and the Palestine Home Guard. Two thousand army orders for land mines, ammunition, and supplies were filled in the factories of Tel Aviv and Haifa. Expanding industries conserved important shipping space by manufacturing hundreds of articles to meet local requirements.

It was in 1945, at the close of the hostilities of World War II, that it became apparent that some sort of change was needed in the Holy Land. The British, the Arabs, and the Jews had different aims. The antagonisms, growing from these conflicting aims, produced simmering undercurrents that at times exploded into physical violence.

By 1947, conditions had deteriorated rather than improved, and the British Government handed the Palestine problem to the United Nations for solution, and declared that they would withdraw from the Holy Land in 1948. The U.N. promptly appointed a Special Committee on Palestine, who examined the situation personally both in Palestine and in Europe and drew up recommendations. These were carefully considered and voted upon at Lake Success. Action taken by the United Nations Assembly on November 29th, 1947, authorized the creation of an independent Jewish State in part of Palestine.

When the British declared that they were withdrawing their troops from Palestine, the armies of five neighboring Arab nations began to filter in across the borders and later marched boldly in, with the declared purpose of driving the Jews into the sea.

Abdul Rahman Azzam Pasha, Secretary General of the Arab League, declared: "This war will be a war of extermination and a momentous massacre, which will be spoken of like the Mongol massacres and the Crusades."

So confident were they of victory, that they gave instructions to the Palestine Arabs to leave their homes in cities and villages so as to be out of the way when the fighting and "liquidation" would take place. Despite statements by the Jews that the Arab inhabitants could remain, a mass exodus took place, part in advance of the fighting and part in hurried flight during operations. There are close to 200,000 Arabs residing today in Israel on a basis of full equality.

The Arab armies made their first attacks on isolated Jewish settlements in Galilee to the north, in the Negev to the south, and those situated in the Judean Hills and the Jordan Valley. The most bitter and prolonged struggle of the war was for Jerusalem and the main highway connecting it with the coast.

The Arabs encountered a solid core of resistance and the tide of battle never once made them victors. What was the secret of Jewish success? Most of all, it was the grim determination to win through or to die fighting. The valor of the young Israeli Jews was matched by that of recent arrivals from the Displaced Persons camps of Europe and by hundreds of volunteers from many countries, non-Jews among them, who found their way to Palestine to play a part for a cause they believed in.

In its Declaration of Independence, the State of Israel declares that the new republic will be based on the precepts of liberty, justice and peace as taught by the Hebrew Prophets, upholding the full social and political equality of all its citizens, without distinction of race, creed, or sex, and guaranteeing full freedom of conscience, worship, education, and culture to all its inhabitants. It undertakes to safeguard the sanctity and inviolability of the shrines and Holy Places of all religions; and dedicates itself to the principles of the Charter of the United Nations.

Efficient operation of all public services was maintained by a Provisional Government until February 14, 1949, when the first democratically elected Knesset Israel, or Constituent Assembly, which included Arabs as well as Jews, was opened in Jerusalem. All citizens who have reached the age of twenty-one are eligible to vote, and members of the Knesset are elected by secret ballot for a period of four years. Members of the Knesset, by secret vote, elect the president of the State for a five-year term, and the president, after consultation with the leaders of the various parties, appoints the Prime Minister, and, upon his advice, the other members of the Executive Council, which includes the heads of all government departments. The President appoints ambassadors and ministers and army officers, but it is the Prime Minister who presides over the meetings of the Executive Council, or Cabinet, and who is responsible for the coordination of activities and the execution of policies adopted by the Executive Council, which, in turn, is responsible to the Knesset. Should the Executive Council cease to retain the support of a majority of the Knesset, it must resign. This government set-up is very similar to that of the British Parliament and French Chamber of Deputies.

Dr. Chaim Weizmann, veteran Zionist leader and world-renowned scientist, was elected the first President, and David Ben-Gurion was named Prime Minister. Hebrew was made the official language of the new state, and its flag is a white banner with two horizontal blue stripes, and the sixpointed star, or Shield of David, in the center. On May 11, 1949, the State of Israel was made the fifty-ninth member of the United Nations.

Peace in Israel is an object lesson to the world of the power of a constructive idea, passionately believed in by a unified people, and fought for with courage and strength. Dr. Chaim Weizmann significantly declared:

"Independence is never given to a people, it has to be earned; and having been earned, it has to be defended.

"It will be our destiny to create institutions and values of a free community in the spirit of the great traditions which have contributed so much to the thought and spirit of mankind."

Upon the death of Dr. Weizmann, on November 9, 1952, the members of the Knesset elected Yitzhak Ben-Zvi, a pioneer worker, scholar and leader, as the second President of Israel.

CHAPTER FOUR

Arab Ways of Adjusting to Life

ⅬⅬⅬⅬⅬⅬⅬⅬⅬⅬⅬⅬⅬⅬⅬ

GLARING sunshine shimmers over empty dunes, but stops at the open flaps of a black, low-swung Beduin tent. Squatting in the shade at one end of the tent is an aged sheikh and half a dozen tribesmen. Their lean, weather-tanned faces are framed by their long white head-scarves, held in place by two circlets of black goat's hair. Dark cloaks, hanging loosely from the shoulders, almost cover their long striped gowns. Opposite them are three men in Western clothes—Jews, who have come to settle on a price for the land that they wish to buy.

Salutations have been courteously exchanged: "Peace to you" and "Unto you peace." Three rounds of black coffee, carrying the pungent aroma of cardamon, have been poured from a small beaked brass coffee-pot into tiny porcelain cups held by each person in the group. And now the Jews bring the conversation around to the proposed purchase. Their spokesman mentions a certain amount. The sheikh smiles but says nothing. The bid is raised, but the sheikh shakes his head. Finally he speaks:

"Don't let us talk about pounds and piastres, buying and selling. This land belonged to the Children of Israel two thousand years ago. It still belongs to you. When the Jews were driven out of Palestine, God looked around for a people to watch over the land until you should return. He selected the Arabs, kin to you, to perform this task. We did not build cities, we did not plant vineyards and orange groves. We were merely watchmen, living in tents. You do not buy land from a watchman. You merely pay him for taking care of the land for you all these hundreds of years."

This little incident took place thirty years ago, when title was transferred for the ground on which the trim little town of Nathania now stands. The Beduin tribesmen were well pleased with the amount of money that passed into their hands. They moved their black tents a little farther down the coast and waited to see what would happen next.

Thirty years ago, the Beduin formed an important part of the population of Palestine. They were nomads who wandered about the deserts and empty plains with herds of camels and flocks of sheep and goats, stopping here and there where the grazing was good. Then there were the Fellahin, farmers who lived in small villages. Some farmers lived in towns, together with artisans and tradesmen. The men who were rich landowners and who had some education were called Effendi.

But time marches on. Until 1919 there wasn't a single motor car in the country. Camels—the main source of income to the Beduin—were the chief means of transport for both men and goods. Today Israel is motor-minded. Buses, cars, and trucks have replaced the four-legged carriers in all but remote districts.

Finding that the camel business was no longer what it used to be, Beduin tribes began to divide up the land allotted to them under a Government land settlement scheme and started planting wheat and barley and lentils. A good many sheikhs still live in tents in the southern part of the land, but some are finding a house more comfortable when they do not have to keep moving around.

The Beduin are often dark-hued from generations of exposure. They are fond of having small dots or designs tattooed on the nose, chin, cheeks, and legs. The women have silver bracelets, rings, and necklaces; and often a fringe of gold or silver coins frames their foreheads or a bunch of old coins is suspended from their headgear, covering their noses. Beduin women wear long, indigo dresses, sometimes with bands of lighter blue at the lower edge. Head-scarves are black or dark maroon squares, which the married woman folds into a band and winds over her hair.

The man's costume consists of a white cotton shirt or Turkish-style pants, bagged at the seat. Over this is worn a striped cotton or tight-fitting silk gabardine, with a leather belt around the waist. Next comes the *aba* or *abeyah*, which may be used as a coat, over-coat, raincoat, or blanket. It hangs loosely from the shoulders, open down the front, and on rainy days is pulled up over the head. A rich sheikh or effendi may have one made of fine camel's hair from Damascus, with gold or silver embroidery around the neck-band—black, orange, or cream-colored, but the ordinary ones are usually dark brown. A poor tribesman or villager may use homespun coarse wool which his wife has woven into cloth and sewed up for him. When an Arab travels at night, he wraps him-self in his abeyah.

Beduin never wear hats or caps. Heads are covered with scarves of a fringed thin material, usually white, but sometimes red and white or black-and-white checked. About a yard square, the scarf is doubled cornerwise and laid on the head with the fold in front. The double coil of black wool or goat's hair which holds the scarf in place is called an *agal*. The scarf, or *kefiyah,* protects the neck and most of the face from the fierce rays of the sun, and may be drawn across the face up to the eyes for protection in a sandstorm.

To Western eyes, the white headscarf and flowing robes are rather romantic, and when the modern Arab goes without them, he loses most of his old-fashioned glamor. Sheikhs and emirs do well to continue their traditional costumes, for, dressed in every-day suits and hats, they would appear as just ordinary Semitic-looking men.

Arab customs, like those of other peoples, are really their way of adjusting to the conditions of life. For protection, the Beduin live in family groups called tribes. This may sound strange to

Americans or Europeans because we are so accustomed to the
State idea, but this organization of society still exists in India and
China, and was found in Europe not so many centuries ago. When
the white men arrived in America, they found the Indians had
their tribal organizations.

The Bible describes how the Land of Canaan was divided
among the twelve tribes of Israel, each tribe tracing its ancestry
back to a different son of Jacob, with Abraham and Isaac common
forefathers. The Jews have kept alive this feeling of descent from
Abraham, Isaac, and Jacob. The Beduin trace their descent from
Ishmael, Abraham's other son. So that makes the Jews and Beduin cousins!

When a Beduin tribe grew too large to travel conveniently
together, it broke up into subdivisions. At times, some of these
subdivisions found it advisable to settle down and cultivate the
soil, and so many Beduin became villagers or Fellahin, as they
are today. Being a clan unit, the land was owned collectively.
For greater security, a clan would welcome other groups, also
organized as clans. Many of these migrations took place generations back, sometimes centuries ago.

Among both Beduin and village clans, the sheikh is the head
of the group. Some sheikhs are young, dark, and handsome, as in
the Hollywood version, but usually they are bearded patriarchs.
The sheikh is more a chief arbitrator than a dictator, as justice in
accordance with time-honored rules is aimed at. A distinction is
made between intentional and unintentional wrong-doing. Of-
fenses against women are severely punished. Members of a clan
obey an elaborate set of rules and regulations which have all the
force of law.

Clans give individuals a sense of "belonging" which is often
conspicuously absent in Western civilization. Members get a feeling of security, for they know that the whole clan will avenge any
wrong done them. They early acquire an understanding of responsibility for their actions, for if anyone steals or murders, the whole
clan will be held accountable. A father or an uncle stands sponsor

for the good behavior of a boy or man convicted of petty wrong-doing.

When a man is convicted of murder, blood-money now takes the place of blood feuds. A truce is declared, and the clan to which the murderer belongs is required to pay a sum of money, the customary rate now being about $1200 per person. Part of this goes to the immediate relatives of the deceased and part to the funds of the clan of which he had been a member. Under a recent ordinance, such compensation, collected from relatives of the offender in proportion to what they can afford, is liable to be paid until the fifth generation. The guilty person must pay double.

Alternatively, a court may order an offender's daughter to be given in marriage to the deceased's son, to remain wedded to him until she bears a son, after which time she may return to her family. It is in this way that the accused's family atone by restoring a life for the life taken.

When a dispute arises between two clans, the leading men of a neighboring clan are called upon to act as judges, and both sides agree to accept the decision.

As a means of livelihood, the Beduin raise and sell camels, sheep, and goats. As they do not wish to go to the bother of raising fodder crops, they feed their herds and flocks on the scanty grass and thorns of the desert. When everything is eaten up in one location, they have to move on. It would not be practical to build a house for a short stay, so they live in tents, which can be folded up and carried by the camels, and then set down again when they arrive at a fresh grazing ground.

Some bright person, back in the dim past, found that threads spun from the shearings of black goats could be woven into a coarse heavy fabric that would afford protection from rain and cold winds, as well as from the intense rays of the sun. To this day, Beduin women keep busy spinning, weaving, and sewing strips of goat's-hair cloth for new tents or to patch up places that have worn out.

The tents are oblong, averaging about eight yards in length and half as wide. Two rows of three long poles hold up the tent. Detachable flaps are used on the sides and ends which, on hot days, may be lifted. A tent is always pitched with its back to prevailing winds. A curtain divides a tent into two sections, one of which belongs to the women. The women's section is also used as the kitchen and the place to store the bedding, the rugs, the copper cooking pots, the food, and the saddlery.

The other side is the living room and guest section. This is where the men sit and talk, and where visitors are entertained. It contains no flooring or furniture, but when guests are expected or sighted in the distance, rugs are laid, and mattresses are spread out at one end of the tent, with cushions and bolsters or camel saddles on which to lean. As a rule, there are no decorations, but wealthy sheikhs sometimes have curtains made of strips of leather and hides, and King Abdullah of Jordan once lined his black tent with crimson satin when he was celebrating his son's wedding by giving a big party for two thousand tribesmen.

The cooking is done in the women's section, but the huge trays of food are brought in for the guests by men servants, and the sheikh himself sees that the guests are well served. Coffee-making, however, is man's prerogative. Sometimes the number of beaked coffee-pots of hand-hammered brass or copper, large and small, may indicate the wealth or standing of their owner. Coffee-making is quite a ceremony, often performed by a black-hued Sudanese former slave, who chants some ancient song while rhythmically pounding the coffee beans in a large wooden mortar with a long-handled pestle. Charcoal embers provide the fuel for the cooking. Coffee is boiled, allowed to settle, poured off, and then boiled again. The final product, flavored with cardamon or coriander seed, is bitter but delicious and thirst-quenching. Only about a thimbleful of this "gahwa" is served at a time in tiny round cups without handles, the size of half an eggshell, but everyone receives at least three rounds of it.

Mint-flavored sweet tea is growing in popularity among the

desert-dwellers, and often the meal is preceded by rounds of coffee and followed by glasses of tea.

Beduin eat meat very seldom. Feasts occur when visitors arrive or the festivals roll around. As the Beduin have no refrigerators, such dinners are always prepared from freshly killed sheep or goats, and served with rice or the roasted grains of wheat, called *burghul*. The main item of diet is bread—large flat pancakes, freshly baked on concave disks of sheet iron, heated by a fire of thorns and brushwood. The sheep and goats provide milk, and from this the women prepare butter, cheese, a refreshing thin sour milk, and buttermilk. *Dibs,* something like dark, thick honey, is made from dates. Onions and olives are kept on hand, and usually there are a few chickens to provide some eggs. Occasionally there are wild artichokes, wild celery, mushrooms, spinach, radishes, tomatoes and cucumbers.

Beduin sheikhs are noted for their gracious hospitality, and many can express themselves with poetic eloquence even when they cannot read or write. The tribesmen compensate for lack of knowledge of the printed word by listening to oft-repeated stories and family traditions, and by exchanging ideas among themselves. On occasions, recitations are given, accompanied by a one-string fiddle, and the program may also include reed-pipe music, singing, and group dancing by the men. In the Beersheba district, camel and horse races used to be popular when harvest fields had been cleared.

With a few exceptions, Beduin tribes are Moslems. Mohammed, the founder of Islam, was born in the Arabian town of Mecca in 570 A.D. He was a camel driver and merchant as a young man, and showed no signs of exceptional character until the age of forty. Then he began to receive visions and became convinced that, like Abraham and Jesus, he was empowered to convey the word of God. The Koran, the Moslem Bible or Gospel, is a collection of sermons and rules of conduct, which Mohammed felt were divinely revealed. He had talked to Jews and Christians in

Arabia and Syria, and many aspects of Judaism and Christianity
were incorporated into the new religion.

Mohammed's message was that all idols must be discarded because there was only one god—Allah. He laid down the axiom
that every Moslem is the brother of every other Moslem, and that
Islam is a brotherhood, a democratic community. Ibrahim (Abraham), Musa (Moses), Da'ood (David), and Issa (Jesus) were hailed
by Mohammed as inspired prophets, and he looked on himself
merely as one of many prophets. His followers, however, called
him the last and the greatest of the prophets of God.

Originally Mohammed decreed Saturday as the Moslem sabbath, forbade the use of pork, and directed the praying Moslem
to turn toward Jerusalem. After the Jews of Medina refused to
recognize him as a new prophet, he changed the day of rest to
Friday and made his followers turn toward Mecca instead of
Jerusalem. But he still kept the taboo on pork.

The typical Arab village in Israel consists of clusters of huts
of sun-dried mud bricks in the plains, and houses of rough-hewn
stone in the hill sections. No trees or gardens add a note of beauty,
no water, gas, or electricity is available in the homes. In fact, no
modern conveniences or sanitary provisions of any kind are to
be found. The houses seem all bunched together on high, stony
ground, with crooked little cobblestone lanes for streets. If you
peer into an entrance, you find the interior dark and unfurnished.

Why build a village in such a crazy-quilt fashion? It was one
way of meeting a problem. Down through the centuries, maraud-
ing bands of Beduin would make sudden raids on tillers of the
soil and carry off whatever they could lay their hands on, or roving
shepherds would lead their flocks into fields of barley and corn.
Building the houses close together afforded some measure of protection in case of attack, and using the most elevated section available meant that the surrounding fields could be watched for the
approach of grazing animals. The jumbled effect is partly due to
the erection of additional homes as families grew larger.

Then too, for the four hundred years of Turkish domination

(1517-1917), and for centuries before that, the only interest of the rulers of the people in this part of their realm had been the extraction of taxes—in produce of the land when money was not available. When the Sultan appointed a pasha to be governor over a district, he was not concerned about how he obtained the revenue, as long as his treasury received the expected amount. The pasha extracted a little extra for himself, if possible a great deal extra. Officials under him had the same idea of finding ways to squeeze the last possible surplus from these peasants, who had no one to whom they could appeal.

Was it any wonder that the poor Arabs often resigned themselves to their fate and said: "It is the will of Allah." The peasants, or Fellahin, soon found that there was little use in having a surplus if it was to be taken away. So they made no attempt to cultivate more and better crops. It did not even seem worthwhile to keep the terrace walls along the hillsides in repair. It was best to hide whatever money a man could obtain for his olives and barley behind a brick in the wall or in a hole in the ground, and to look for all possible ways to avoid the tax collector.

The lessons learned through the bitter experiences of a thousand years are not laid aside at once. Our ideas of public health and free education have been evolving through the ages. Labor standards, emancipation of women, and social insurance have been accepted in very limited parts of the world, and only after a gradual changing of public opinion. It is asking a lot to expect the illiterate, impoverished Arab fellahin to grasp the modern world and its current ideas all at once.

The real surprise comes when the outsider sees that happiness and contentment are not necessarily bound up with bathtubs and telephones. The Arab women may go barefoot out of choice rather than from necessity. She may not enjoy having her feet confined in hot, ill-fitting shoes. When she goes to the well to draw water, the neighbor's gossip that she hears may more than compensate her for the trip back and forth. When she is satisfied with the often meager leavings from the meal of the men in the family, it has not occurred to her that any other way would be in order. Many of the villages are so remote that even today life goes on according to the routine set by the customs of other centuries.

Due to the lack of public security even fifty years ago, the house had to be used for the protection of the few animals the family might possess and for the storage of supplies. The houses usually consist of one large square room, with a walled-in little courtyard in front. In primitive houses, only the front third of the room is on ground-level. The rest is raised from three to ten feet and is reached by rudely constructed steps which lead to a sort of masonry platform. Here, at night, mattresses are spread out for the family. In the morning, the mattresses are rolled up, together with the blankets or quilts, and stacked in arched niches in the walls. No beds are used. Neither are tables and chairs. The villagers squat crosslegged on the floor. Often a bridal chest is the only article of furniture. When no chest is available, dresses are hung over a cord stretched across a corner of the room.

At night, the lower level houses the chickens, the goats or sheep, and sometimes even a cow or donkey. A number of boxlike containers built of clay (*khabieh*), slightly raised off the floor, hold the family's supply of barley, wheat, and millet. Close by is the animal fodder and the brushwood for the fire. A clay baking-oven (*taboon*) is usually located in a corner of the courtyard.

When the house has a flat roof, this is often used as a place on which to dry tomatoes, figs, and raisins. It also affords a cooler sleeping place on summer evenings than the overcrowded common room. A flight of stairs outside the house, usually without any railing, leads to the roof. It is customary, when a new house is being put up, for all the men in the village to lend a hand with the roof, and the completion of the house is celebrated with a feast.

Not all village homes are so primitive. In some of the larger villages, tiles are used for flooring and no animals are lodged in the house. Occasionally a few chairs may be owned and brought out for special guests. Sometimes a wardrobe has been acquired. When the family has some town connection or has risen above the average by wealth or education, overstuffed sofas and chairs have been purchased. These are always lined against the walls of the living-room.

In addition to his village home, a man may have a summer cottage up the mountain near his vineyard. This resembles a small Eskimo igloo, only it is built of loose stones, with a few branches for a roof. Again no furniture, merely a place to eat and sleep. A near-by cave may serve as kitchen and storage room. How simple and uncomplicated life can be, comments the visitor used to all the gadgets of civilization!

Let us get acquainted with Salim and Jameela, aged twelve and ten. They are the youngest children in a big family. The family includes not only older brothers and sisters, but grandparents, many uncles and aunts, and lots of cousins. Half the village is related to them. Almost all the people who live in the village were born there, and very few ever think of moving away.

Next door live their grandparents. Both families use the same oven for baking bread. Jameela gets up early and watches her mother mix a little water and flour, and a pinch of salt, in a wooden bowl, and then knead the dough until it is soft and elastic. A portion is then flattened out and made thinner and thinner by expertly tossing it from one hand to the other before flopping it into the oven. When baked, this flattish bread, called *pitta,* is about ten inches in diameter, and tastes especially good when eaten warm. It is a bit thicker than the bread baked by the Beduin. The oven is usually big enough to bake six loaves. While the bread is baking, the mother milks the sheep and goats.

Sometimes Salim and Jameela help their mother gather brambles and thorns from the hillsides for fuel. The manure from their sheep and goats and donkey is also dried and used for fuel, as coal and wood are seldom obtainable.

Jameela has learned how to balance a clay jar or a gasoline-tin full of water on her head. Not directly on top of her head, for she rests her load on a little roll of twisted cloth which she places under her head-shawl. Girls are kept pretty much at home, so it is always a treat for Jameela to accompany her mother to the village spring for water. Sometimes the family washing is taken along, and then Jameela helps to pound out the dirt on flat stones after applying soap.

Salim and Jameela have never been to the movies, but their parents and grandparents have told them many wonderful stories. They have heard them so many times that they almost know them by heart. These stories contain sayings, maxims, precepts, and proverbs which have been handed down from one generation to the next for hundreds of years.

Jameela is often busy learning how to embroider a dress for herself. She would not think of wearing a dress without solid embroidery down the front of the waist, and more embroidery on the sleeves. Her dresses are almost exactly like those worn by her mother and her aunts. Her mother can tell at a glance what part of the country a woman comes from by the combination of colors and designs on her dress. Usually, black silk or sateen is the material used, but the women of one district prefer white cotton with inserts of red, yellow and green, and those of another section use white linen when it can be obtained.

The dress, called a *tobe,* is made with one width of cloth for the front and another for the back. A girdle wound around the waist allows the dress to be bloused a little. Of course the girls and women have best dresses set aside for special occasions, but they wear these lovely costumes for everyday work too, folding back the long loose sleeves when they do the washing. How they manage to keep them so clean is a mystery.

Jameela has her own head-scarf too, not quite as big as her mother's, but made out of the same thin, white material. She folds it just as she has seen her mother do, so that it falls gracefully down the sides of her face. She knows that this scarf can come in handy some day when she needs a basket or a bag. She has seen others spread out the scarf, place the things that are to be carried in the center of the square, tie the ends together, and balance it all on the head.

Jameela and her cousins spend pleasant afternoons learning how to make pretty baskets and trays of fine straw selected from the grain and dyed red and green and blue and orange.

Salim too is kept busy with many things to see and learn to do. He helps his father yoke two oxen together for the plowing. If two oxen cannot be borrowed, perhaps it will be two mules. Often his father uses a single horse or a camel to pull the plow. The plow only scratches the surface of the ground, sinking in but a few inches. It is made of wood, with a metal tip. Salim knows that soon after the first rainstorms moisten the parched land in November, his father will let him help in scattering grains of wheat, barley, and lentils for the winter crops.

Next comes the time to plow the ground around the vineyards and the olive trees, and also the fields reserved for the summer crops. When the top crust of the earth is loosened by the plow, the rain has a better chance to sink in and be stored up for the crops which are planted after the last rains fall in April. Durra and millet, watermelons and cantaloupes and tomatoes all grow in the summer with no water from above except the morning dew. In every village, the winter crop zone and the summer crop area are interchanged each year to keep the soil in good condition. This is called crop rotation.

When harvest time comes, the men are glad to have the help of the boys and the women. These Arab farmers do not have motor-driven reapers that mow down the crops. The grain is cut, a little at a time, with a knife or sickle, and tied into small bundles. These bundles are collected and loaded on donkeys and camels, and sometimes on the heads of the women, and carried to a threshing-floor in the neighborhood, a *joren*—a hard, flat piece of ground. In former times, the tax collector chose a portion of the grain and had it threshed and delivered to him before the rest of the work was allowed to proceed.

Threshing is a picturesque but very primitive and time-consum-

ing affair. The sheaves of grain are spread over the threshing-
floor and the grain is beaten out. This is accomplished by driving
teams of cattle or horses round and round over the sheaves after
the animals have been shod with special iron shoes for the purpose. The straw is stirred up with wooden forks after the animals
pass by. The process is repeated time and again until the straw
is thoroughly chopped up.

Now comes the winnowing. The trampled grain is tossed high
into the air with a wooden fork and the grain kernels fall straight
down, while the chaff is blown to one side. A slight wind is important to carry off the chaff, so the winnowing often takes place at
sunset or in the moonlight when the right amount of wind is
present. A sieve is used to separate the coarse stubble that hasn't
blown away. This stubble, or *tibben* as it is called, is saved and
used as a fodder for the animals. Finally, the grain is placed in
sacks and divided among the owners, if several families have
worked together.

The Bible tells us that it was on the site of a threshing-floor
which King David bought from the Jebusites that the holy
Temple in Jerusalem was erected.

Salim has decided that when he gets bigger, he will wear a red
tarbush, like the one his uncle wears. This is a felt fez, or flat-
domed hat, with a dark blue tassel that hangs toward one side.
His father wears a turban, but Salim thinks this a little old-fashioned. Still, he likes to watch his father make his turban by winding a large square of silk or wool or cotton around an old tarbush,
and it seems wonderful to him how the folds come into position
and the ends get tucked in just right.

A man's turban tells the world quite a bit about him, just as
a woman's dress shows what section of the country she comes from.
If he has made a pilgrimage to Mecca, he is privileged to wear a
snow-white turban. A plain green turban proclaims the wearer a
direct descendant of the Prophet Mohammed. There are more
of these descendants than you might imagine—literally thousands
of them. A dervish or a holy man wears plain red. In the district

north of Jerusalem, a colored border woven into white linen is preferred. Around Hebron, the popular choice is yellow and red. In a crowd, the colors of turbans are so varied that you wonder if the striking contrasts just happen by chance or come about through a primitive love of bright shades. Villagers also wear the white head-scarves in the same fashion as the Beduin.

Salim has been wearing a long striped gabardine, red and yellow, or black and yellow, but he has noted that one of his uncles often wears a jacket instead of an abeyah for a coat over his gabardine. That seems to be more practical for the village grain store where his uncle works. Mustapha, one of his older brothers, who is a post-office employee, has begun to wear a regular coat and trousers, and Salim thinks that this style will be best for him too in a couple of years.

Now let us listen in on a little conversation between this Mustapha and his father. The father says:

"Mustapha, you're almost twenty years old—time you were getting married. I've been saving up some money to pay for a bride for you, and I think I've found the right girl. Your grandparents will go live with your uncle Tewfig, and you and Tamara can have their house, right next door."

"Tamara?" falters Mustapha, "you mean little Tamara, my cousin?"

"Who else? Have you noticed how nicely she is growing up? Your mother tells me that she bakes good bread and that her embroidery is something to boast about. You haven't any other girl in mind, have you?" asks the father, for he is kind and doesn't want to force his son against his will.

"No, there is no one else. I think Tamara will be all right. I have seen her going for water to the spring, and she seems strong and good-looking."

"Fine," says the father. "I will speak to her father and arrange for your betrothal."

Among the Moslems, husband and wife get acquainted after marriage, not before. Their relatives and friends expect them to get along well, and usually they do. A girl is lucky if she gets a young man for a husband. Often an elderly widower likes to have a young girl of sixteen for a wife, and if the father of the girl consents, there is nothing for the girl to do but obey. In former years, girls were married as early as twelve or thirteen, but such child-marriages seldom occur now.

In the United States and Great Britain, many parents select the college to which their children go, and the children accept their decision, and also their advice about business and professional careers. Among the Arabs in Israel this parental advice goes one step further—to the choice of a wife or husband. Marriage there means the carrying on of the family traditions with the establishment of a new home, and it seems logical for cousins to marry one another. The bride becomes a part of her husband's family.

Sometimes it is not so easily arranged as indicated in the conversation between Mustapha and his father. The son may have seen or heard of a wonderful girl in another village whom he would like to marry. No courtship is permitted between young men and girls. They do not even play together as children. So it becomes the job of the mother of the young man to look the girl over. She goes to see the girl, accompanied by her daughters and a few women friends. If her report is satisfactory, the men in the family make the next step. Father, son, and uncles proceed to the village for a visit to the girl's family, and a formal request is made for the girl's hand in marriage.

The father of the prospective bridegroom must pay a certain amount of money to the father of the girl. Some fathers demand more money than others, depending mostly on the position of the family, on the girl's beauty, her age, and her skill in cooking. Though one speaks of the price "paid for the bride," the sum handed over is partly spent for the bride's outfit, which includes dresses and veils and jewelry, a mattress, pillows, and a quilt. Usually there is quite a bit left over which the father may keep for himself. So, among the Arabs, the father of daughters does not have to worry about dowries. He actually makes money when his daughters marry. Nevertheless, every father rejoices more over the birth of a son than the arrival of a daughter. Thirty years ago, the average price paid for a village bride was $100 to $400, but now the cost has gone up for this as for everything else.

Considerable conversation goes on about the exact price to be paid when the formal request for the girl is made. If the suitor is not acceptable, the father demands a price which he knows will not be given. This is a polite form of refusal. If the final offer is accepted, the details of the betrothal contract are arranged and a feast concludes the day's activities. The sheep for the feast are provided by the prospective bridegroom's father. The girl may never have seen her future husband. She is not consulted as a rule.

The engaged man is expected to present the bride's mother with a new dress, and her father and her eldest uncles with new cloaks or abeyahs. He also gives a present to the clubhouse of the bride's village and is host at a couple of feasts for the villagers.

Wedding festivities last a whole day and sometimes for several days or a week, with the men entertaining themselves in the clubhouse with dancing and feasting, while the women gather in the home of the bridegroom. The rhythm for the dancing is provided by hand-clapping or the beating of a tom-tom.

The wedding contract, containing the names of both parties, the amount paid for the bride, and other details, is carefully signed by the bridegroom and the bride's representative—usually her father or her nearest male relative, in the presence of the Imam, the religious head of the village. There is no formal wedding ceremony in which the bride takes part, but there is a grand procession when the bride leaves her home to go to that of the bridegroom.

Moslem law permits a man to have four wives if he can support them. The great majority find that one at a time is quite enough. In a study made in five Arab villages during Mandate days, of 566 married men, sixty had more than one wife. Fifty-six had two wives, three had three wives each, and one man had four wives.

Sometimes the first wife really prefers her husband to take a second wife rather than divorce her and leave her stranded. The new wife is usually provided with a separate room or another house. When men or women are divorced or lose their marriage partners by death, they usually remarry.

Social life for men in an Arab village centers in the *madafe* or guest house. Here the men gather in the late afternoon or early evening, or during the entire day if they have nothing else to do, and talk over the news which someone may have brought from the nearest town or neighboring village. They exchange the latest gossip and complain about the weather. The boys stop in, too, and it is by listening attentively to the men in the madafe that Salim and Mustapha and Achmed learn about the world and the forces that run it, what succeeds and what fails, about the traditions of the village, and local politics. If someone should happen to bring a newspaper from the city, few could read it. Most of the news is obtained from someone who has read the paper and passed on the information to others. By the time it is repeated in the madafe, much of it may be inaccurate. A more reliable source of information is the radio loudspeaker, which may be in operation in some of the villages. The Israel Government broadcasts music, and the news and agricultural advice in Arabic.

If there is more than one clan in a village, each clan has its own madafe. Individual homes do not as a rule have any accommodation for the entertainment of company, so if a man has a visitor, he takes him over to the madafe. The villagers take turns in keeping the little one-roomed house in order and in keeping it supplied with coffee, sugar, rice, barley, and other foods as needed. If a stranger is entertained overnight—and every traveler is hospitably welcomed without charge, the host for the day furnishes food and bedding.

Eggs, bread, and olives, and perhaps a bowl of *leben* (clabbered milk) may be offered the ordinary traveler, but if the visitor is an important person, the meal may include chicken and rice.

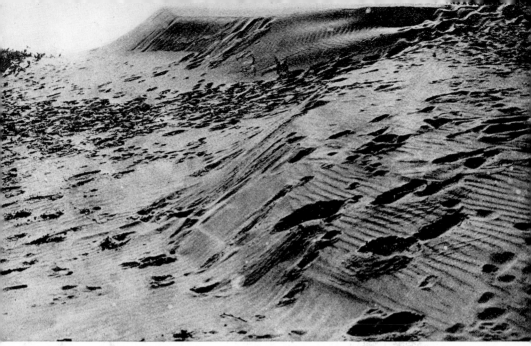

The site of Tel Aviv in 1909

The beach front in Tel Aviv today

MEDITERRANEAN SEA

MT. HERMON

LEBANON
KFAR GILADI
HANITA
EILON
LAKE HULEH
NAHARIA
SAFED
GALILEE
ROSH PINAH
ACRE
GINOSAR
CAPERNAUM
HAIFA BAY
RAMAT YOCHANAN
SEA OF GALILEE
HAIFA
KISHON
TIBERIAS
EIN GEB
MT. CARMEL
YAGUR
NAZARETH
KINNERET
THE EMEK
YARMUK R.
MEGIDDO
MT. TABOR
DEGANIA
EIN HAROD
AFIKIM
ASHDOT YAACOV
TEL YOSEF
PARDESS HANNA
BETH ALPHA
BEISAN
GAN SHMUEL
HEDERA
JENIN
SHARON
NATHANIA
JERASH
NABLUS
JORDAN R.
TEL AVIV
PETACH TIKVAH
JAFFA
BAT YAM
RISHON le ZION
RAMALLAH
REHOVOT
GIVAT BRENNER
JERICHO
JERUSALEM
MT. NEBO
BEIT JALLAH
BETHLEHEM
LACHISH
DEAD SEA
MOAB
R. ARNON
ISRAEL
BEERSHEBA
KERAK
MT. JEBEL USDUM

EGYPT

THE
NEGEV

SYRIA

JORDAN

PETRA

0 5 10 15 20 25 30 35 40 45 50

AQABA

TURKEY
SYRIA
IRAQ
CYPRUS
LEBANON
BAGHDAD
(MESOPOTAMIA)
JORDAN
JERUSALEM
EGYPT
SINAI PEN.

0   100   200   300   400

The approach to Jerusalem with the Garden of Gethsemane in foreground

The Western or Wailing Wall in Jerusalem

The Via Dolorosa in Jerusalem

Y.M.C.A. Building in Jerusalem

G. ERIC MATSON

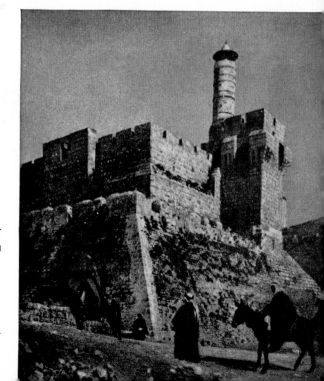

The citadel and Tower
of David, Jerusalem

Y. BENOR-KALTER

Kingsway in Haifa, chief port of Israel

Pioneers on the southern shore of the Dead Sea

Part of the Jordan Valley

Fish ponds in agricultural settlements

A kibbutz in the Judean hills

A camel pulls a primitive plow

Fertile fields replace the wastelands

Potash and other chemicals
extracted from the waters
of the Dead Sea

Y. BENOR-KALTER

Rachel's Tomb

A swimming pool in Kibbutz Ginegar, with Mt. Tabor in the distance

Cliffs and sea meet
at Nathania

SIGMUND H. STEINBERG

Up the winding road to Safed

The Jordan flowing into the Dead Sea

Tiberias on the Sea of Galilee

Young fishermen on the banks of the Jordan

Village and hills near Jerusalem

Excavations at Jericho

GAIL HOFFMAN

School children at work in their gardens

Roadmakers

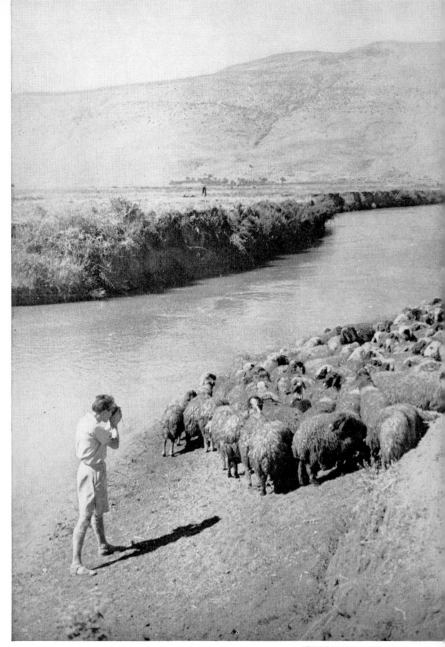

The Jordan Valley is a photographer's paradise

A Mazkir of Kibbutz Ginegar

School children observing the Seder rites

Mealtime in a communal nursery

First President of Israel, Chaim Weizmann

An Arab village

A Beduin gathering

Degania, the oldest of the kibbutzim

Bethlehem

Nazareth

Church of the Holy Sepulchre
in Jerusalem

Dizengoff Circle, Tel Aviv

Students leaving the
Max Pine Trade School

Below: Northern Galilee
looking toward Mt. Hermon

Hanita, a picturesque northern outpost

A street
scene in
Hebron

A young agriculturalist
at Ramat Hakovesh

The flower fields at Mishmar Hasharon

Should a large number of men arrive, or the guest be a sheikh or a high government official, a lamb or a kid may be hastily slaughtered and prepared, and the leading men of the clan are invited to join the party. If the traveler arrives on a horse or donkey, the animal is housed and fed, also without cost.

Welcoming the traveler used to be a necessity in days when no hotels were available and, no matter how limited the villagers' resources, this tradition still survives.

Partaking of a feast is a serious business in a Beduin tent or a Fellahin village. The lack of eating utensils does not by any means indicate an absence of etiquette. There are rules of good form when eating with your fingers as when using the proper fork or spoon. Even the way one sits on the floor is an indication of good breeding. It is offensive to Arabs to have a person sit with his feet stretched out in front of him, exposing the soles of his feet or his shoes. It is extremely bad form to use the left hand in eating. Smacking the lips is taken to indicate appreciation of the food. Hands must be washed before digging into the common bowl or platter.

The most important men group themselves around the huge dish for the first sitting. When they have eaten their fill, others take their places and eat what is left. There is little variety in a feast. The platter is lined with pieces of bread, on which are heaped piles of gleaming white rice, and on this are placed pieces of roasted or boiled lamb, mutton, or kid, with liver, heart, and kidneys arranged on top. Each person reaches out and takes what he wants. The rice is worked into little balls with the right hand and flipped into the mouth by adroit movements of the thumb and first two fingers. This flipping of food into the mouth prevents any direct contact with a person's mouth and the hand that reaches into the common dish.

One of the features of clan organization in Arab villages in the past was the common ownership of land. In order to be fair to each individual family, the area was divided into small plots every two years, and each family received a piece of good land and some that was less desirable. In most villages, there is an area near the spring where most of the vegetables requiring water are grown. Each family has a little section here which the women look after. The olive groves are off in one direction, the vineyards are scattered here and there on the hillsides, and the wheat and barley are planted whenever possible in the fields, sometimes at a distance from the village.

This method of land distribution worked out well enough when the land was cultivated cooperatively, but see what has happened in recent years when, due to government land settlement regulations, the land was permanently divided and registered under individual ownership. A man owned little strips of land in each of these areas so he could have his own vegetables, olives, grapes, and grain. When he died and his property was divided among his sons, the strips grew smaller, and when the next generation received their holdings, the strips were smaller yet. Today, the fellah or farmer wastes a lot of time going from one part of his land to the next part, and very small-scale farming is uneconomic. Even if he wanted to use agricultural machinery, it would hardly be worthwhile on tiny areas. The peasants in India and China suffer the ill-effects of this strip-farming which came about in those countries too because of the original common ownership of land.

In ever increasing number, the Arab villages in Israel contain Government schools, with Arabic the language of instruction, and Government clinics, in addition to the homes, small shops and cafés, mosques, and madafes. The Government of Israel aims to provide education and medical facilities to all its citizens. Arab women as well as men voted in the first general election of the new State, and sent three representatives to the *Kenesset*, or General Assembly.

It will be interesting to observe, as the years go by, how the Arabs of Israel will move toward more modern ideas of living and working while still preserving many of their traditional customs. An important start was made during the thirty years of the British Mandatory Government. During the first three years of Sir Herbert Samuel's term of office as first High Commissioner for Palestine, an average of one new Arab school per week was maintained. At the termination of the British Mandate, four hundred Government schools, with Arabic as the language of instruction, had been established. This meant that most of the Arab boys living in towns and cities had a chance at some schooling, but only fifty percent of the village boys attended classes, and for only four or five years; while but five percent of the village girls received any education.

Providing teachers for the girls' schools in Arab villages was a difficult problem, as a town-bred teacher was seldom willing or capable of meeting primitive village conditions. So a special Women's Rural Teachers' Training Center was set up in Ramallah in 1935, in which Arab village girls equipped themselves with information which they later shared with the women and girls of their own localities. Practical training was given them in housecraft, laundry work, gardening, poultry keeping, cooking and needlework, sewing and baby care, as well as instruction in academic subjects.

The Government also trained hundreds of Arab women as nurses and midwives and started a splendid system of rural public health work in Arab villages. A remarkable reduction in the infant mortality rate was the result.

School gardens in Palestine are not just plots of ground outside the schoolhouse in which a few flowers and vegetables are grown. They are miniature farms which make important demonstration areas for the surrounding districts. Each one carries on interesting experiments and projects. Some specialize in growing seedlings and saplings of subtropical trees, such as the anona, guava, fugia, and loquat. Corn, wheat, and beans are grown in different ways and with a number of varieties of seeds. Tomatoes and grapes are grown on various kinds of support, or allowed to trail on the ground—so everyone can see the comparative results obtained.

Most of the produce of the school garden is marketed and the money used for current expenses, but in the top classes each boy is allowed to cultivate a fifty-yard plot as his own, and he can take home what he produces. Very often proud fathers boast at the village meetings of what their sons have done and the whole community takes a real interest in the gardens. Part of the teacher's job is to extend the knowledge of better agricultural methods throughout the district. Lettuce, spinach, asparagus, artichokes, and even potatoes, now widely used by Arabs, were often tried for the first time when brought home by a boy from a school garden.

Going to school is by no means the only way to learn new ways of doing things. Good roads and motor buses make it possible for people living in remote villages to travel about and observe modern methods and the changes that have come about. Good prices for agricultural products and opportunities for employment have brought money into the hands of Arab villagers. When they go to town, they find locally manufactured goods readily obtainable. When they see the sparkling lights in the agricultural settlements which they pass on their way home after marketing their vegetables, they talk over a plan of bringing electricity to their own homes.

"Why not?" they ask. "These Jews are only simple farmers—and yet they have electric lamps and radios. It would be a fine thing for us in our village too."

CHAPTER FIVE

Israel Blazes New Trails

ⅬⅬⅬⅬⅬⅬⅬⅬⅬⅬⅬⅬⅬⅬⅬⅬⅬⅬⅬⅬⅬⅬ

THE STORY of the building of a Jewish State is exciting because of the great number of difficulties that have had to be overcome, and the many that still lie ahead.

There were always many who said:

"This can't be done. It's quite impossible."

And then, through careful planning and a great deal of hard work, it actually gets done in a surprisingly short time. Then people say:

"A modern miracle!"

Lack of sufficient money was one of the first big difficulties. Work on a large scale needed funds. Land had to be bought, houses erected, farms and factories started. Theodor Herzl in 1897 wanted $50,000,000 to begin with. This seems a very small sum today when you visualize reclamation and housing projects for a whole country. But it took the Zionists many, many years to raise the first $50,000,000.

Ten years later only $300,000 had been raised for the National Fund and only three small pieces of land had been bought. Meanwhile many eager young men and a few young women had come to Palestine and were finding it difficult to obtain work. The Jewish settlers, who had already started farms and orange plantations and vineyards, frequently hired Arabs at low wages in preference to these young, inexperienced immigrants. Something had to be done to help the young people get a start.

The three pieces of land were large enough for only a few families, but if individuals worked together and lived as a little community, many more could be taken care of. That is how the *kibbutzim,* the agricultural communal settlements, originated.

Training centers were opened at Ben Shemen and Hulda, and the third tract of land—on the southeastern shore of the Sea of Galilee—was placed at the disposal of a group of ten young men who had formed a little cooperative while working for others. Banded together, they were not so lonely in a strange land and they could discuss their common problems.

The little group started out bravely. They found a ruined Arab khan (an inn) on the place, in which to live, and they plowed the fields from dawn to dusk, in spite of extremely hot weather. The Sea of Galilee is 686 feet below sea level. The temperature often rises to 110° F. Insufficient food and malaria undermined their health, and the Beduin came down from the hills and set fire to their grain on the threshing floor.

Another group of six men and one woman took up the work when conditions proved too much for the first ten. A year later, these had to be replaced by still others—this time by ten men and two women. Little by little they gained experience. Slowly they were able to extend their fields and grow in numbers.

That was the beginning of the settlement of Dagania—now over forty years old and the pride of the whole land. Acres of fertile fields, barns full of high-grade cattle, rows of neat houses among fine old trees planted by the first settlers, a large dining hall, a library and exhibition hall, a high school and an amphitheatre overlooking the lake. It all seems perfect and well-arranged. And yet if hard work and persistence had not triumphed over repeated failure and disappointment and difficulties, Dagania would never have existed.

With the small funds at their disposal, the Zionists could not afford to buy fertile land or olive groves. Knowing that the Jews wanted land, the Arabs raised their prices to fantastic levels.

Many a piece was offered at $3,000, though it had previously been valued at $300. So the Zionists purchased black swamps, infested with malaria mosquitoes, and empty dunes, and they didn't mind when the Arabs laughed at the idea of paying good money for such poor bargains. Today, the Jewish workers remember that it was they themselves who drained the swamps and so made possible the establishment of hundreds of flourishing agricultural settlements and towns. Through the years, individuals as well as the National Fund gradually increased their holdings.

A second enormous difficulty was the lack of training for work in Palestine. Many of the early pioneers came from schools and universities and shops. What did they know about constructing roads, building houses, planting fields, and milking cows? However, they were young and enthusiastic. They learned. They improved through practice. No work was beyond them. They were called *halutzim*—a special type of hardy pioneer. They organized a General Federation of Labor that trained groups for road and house construction and also obtained contracts for this kind of work.

Word was sent to the young people in Europe who wanted to come to Palestine to prepare themselves by a year or two of training. Groups of men and girls went from Poland and Lithuania to farms in Holland and Denmark to learn dairying and cheese-making. Zionist committees bought small farms in whatever country they happened to be and opened training centers. In addition to farm work, they learned a trade. They gained experience in cooking for large numbers and in making the adjustments necessary to living in a group. They studied Hebrew.

The workers realized that their agricultural settlements would not be a success until they made more money than they spent, so for many years they got along with very simple meals and sent their milk and cream, their eggs and vegetables to market. Now most of the well-established Kibbutzim set aside a certain part of their budget for the repayment of loans, and their meals are satisfactory, though far from being elaborate.

The early pioneers found that they could grow more if they had more water. They dug wells; they irrigated vegetable fields with sprays of water from small pipes which could be moved from place to place; they built reservoirs to hold the rain water. Water companies were organized to drill wells and install pumps, and geologists searched for the best places in which to reach the underground water. In 1940, the Jewish Agency for Palestine established a Water Research Bureau which called in leading American engineers to survey the whole water problem.

The young farmers soon discovered that they could grow more crops if they had better seeds, more fertilizer, and modern farm machinery. There was much more for them to understand about soil conditions and the rotation of crops. So a number of young men went to California to study modern methods and came back and showed the others what they had learned. Some attended the Mikveh Israel Agricultural School which had been started in Palestine back in 1870. The Jewish Agency set up an Agricultural Experiment Station at Rehovot, and the Hebrew University established a Department of Agriculture. They learned what they could from the Arabs and the Government Agricultural Department officials. They read the latest farm journals and did a great deal of experimenting themselves. During the war, when they could not import farm machinery, they made it themselves in their own workshops.

After years of experimentation with growing better seeds, the farmers have concentrated their efforts in an Institute for Seed Cultivation, which produces thousands of tons of seeds annually at special seed farms and nurseries at Ramat Yochanan and Beth Alpha. Research continues for new kinds and varieties.

There was a great deal to be learned about the dairy industry. The cows which the Arabs owned were small and scrawny, and did not give much milk. The newcomers imported some fine Holsteins and Jerseys and, by cross breeding, developed cows which give more milk and still stand the climate. Fine bulls are very costly, so the Cattle Breeders Association made a study of artificial insemination of cattle, and applied the new methods. They realized how important it is for barns to be kept scrupulously clean, for milk to be pasteurized and bottled in sanitary fashion. All this gradual development of the dairy industry meant a lot of hard work, but by 1944 the milk production figures showed that it had produced worthwhile results. Milk produced by 210,000 cows owned by Arabs amounted to 45 million quarts of milk, while the Jewish farmers, though they possessed only 30,000 cows, obtained 60 million quarts of milk.

Instead of growing only one crop of vegetables a year, the new settlers found that they could grow two crops, and, in districts like the Jordan Valley, three and four. They discovered that they could get higher prices for fruits and vegetables if the quality was uniformly high, so they concentrated on growing the best and packed them with care.

How was each farmer or little group of farmers to send the milk and butter, the eggs and fresh vegetables to market in towns and cities? That difficult problem, like so many others, was solved by cooperation, by working together. Farmers in the United States have the same problem, and a great many have joined growers' cooperatives or associations. In Israel today, over ninety percent of the workers in the agricultural communal settlements and seventy percent of the Jewish farmers who own their own farms are members of the Israel Federation of Labor.

This Federation has a central marketing organization called TNUVA. It collects and sells the agricultural and dairy products of its members and divides the profits. By maintaining high standards, it has built up a wonderful reputation. It has wholesale depots and retail outlets. It has erected central dairy plants for bottling milk and preparing different kinds of cheese. It has an export department which ships delicious orange-blossom honey to many countries, and is planning to send winter-grown vegetables to Europe and England by airplane.

The Labor Federation has also developed a buying cooperative organization, known as Hamashbir Hamerkazi, which has grown and prospered under good management. This company supplies fodder, seeds, farm implements, paint, nails, and many other such items, as well as food and clothing. All these may be bought much cheaper when purchased in large quantities, and again the profits are divided among the members, as in all cooperatives.

The kibbutzim or communal farms range in size from Ein Harod and Tel Yosef, each with 3,000 acres, to areas no bigger than 200 or 300 acres. Their numbers vary also. Ein Harod has a thousand members. So do Givat Brenner and Yagur. But most are groups of three, four, or five hundred persons. A few have less than a hundred members.

Most groups are established on land provided by the Jewish National Fund, and money needed for a start comes in the form of a loan, with a very low rate of interest, from the Israel Foundation Fund.

The young people, most of whom are in their early twenties when they start a group, manage everything themselves. There are no supervising elders around. Committees are elected to arrange the various classifications of work, and tasks are assigned to each member of the little community. Most of them have taken special training to fit themselves for a side line in addition to agricultural work. Some go to the barns, others to the fields and orchards and vineyards. A few lead the sheep to pasture. Some must remain at work on administrative duties connected with quantity buying, the storing of food, and the care of the children, the aged, and the sick.

Some settlements have spacious dining halls and modernly equipped kitchens, but often when a group starts operations, the end of a shack, which serves as a dining hall, is partitioned off, a few small paraffin stoves and plain tables are installed, and the kitchen is ready. Yet satisfactory meals must be served on time to hundreds of hungry workers.

Then take the laundry problem. Which of these eager young men and girls would choose to stand over a washtub day after day? And just imagine the socks that have to be darned for the entire group, and the shoes that have to be repaired! These are all jobs to be done, and the men share them with the girls, just as the girls take their part in the work in barn and field.

There is no strict uniformity in wearing apparel. Individual preferences are met as far as possible. If a member of a group is in need of a coat or a pair of shoes, he goes to the storeroom and finds out what is available, or he asks the head of the buying committee to keep his wishes in mind when next she goes to the city on a shopping expedition.

To enable the mother as well as the father to put in a full day's work, trained baby experts and kindergarten teachers take full charge of the young babies and children. Special provisions are made for the mother before and after the birth of her child. The babies and children—always the pride of every settlement—are given the best of everything in housing, food, and clothing, even if the older folks have to do without. Furniture and bathrooms in the houses designed for very young children are suited to the needs of the youngsters. Flowers, pictures, and toys are chosen to provide a cheerful and happy environment. After work, both mothers and dads arrive to spend a happy hour or two with their offspring, and parents spend much of the Sabbath with their children.

Many groups supplement their income from fields and dairies and citrus groves by establishing workshops and factories. This combination of industrial work and agricultural activity is an important development in rural life. It helps to provide employment for every type of member of the groups and makes possible a substantial income during the slack seasons on the farms. Ashdot Yaacov, in the Jordan Valley, maintains large plants for the production of orange concentrate, grapefruit juice, and marmalade. Its neighbor, Afikim, has a large ply-wood factory. Givat Brenner makes useful articles and toys from olive wood and other timber. Eilon, on the northern border, has a big plant for making agricultural machinery. Several have automobile repair shops and tile factories. A number spin wool and produce hand-woven cloth.

This life on the soil, with all its hardships, is what these young people have eagerly selected. They are taking part in a great movement of redeeming a land. No place for pettiness, egotism, or selfishness. They find that the new freedom means discipline. Strict discipline. Immediate and uncomplaining discipline. But they, themselves, work out their own rules and regulations—they are not imposed by others. To these young men and women, cooperative living has provided a means of training in agricultural work, but it is far more than a mere makeshift—it has become a way of life.

Visitors sometimes wonder how the members of the Kibbutzim are happy without spending-money, bank accounts, or expensive personal possessions, how the girls get along without the latest style in dress. These things are unimportant to these young people compared to the sense of self-fulfilment, the feeling that they are successful as tillers of the soil.

The acquisition of another cow, the erection of a new barn, the starting of a canning plant, the buying of a tractor—these are all bricks in the construction of the national home. Each new settlement, the erection of another row of houses, the launching of another boat, is hailed by the entire *Yishuv* (community) as part of a collective enterprise.

In these extracts from diaries kept by boys and girls in the settlement of Kinnereth, on the shores of the Sea of Galilee, you can glimpse what the teen-agers, who had fled from the Nazi terror in Europe, were thinking about as they became adjusted to their new surroundings:

Miriam wrote: "The first Spring in Israel is the first Spring of my life, because here I feel that nature blooms through work. How pleasant is the feeling when we know that Kinneret is developing from our work."

Benjamin expressed himself thus: "Much has my land given to me and much will I give to the land. In spite of the fact that life is difficult here, I cannot imagine living in any other place. In a kibbutz there is no dogma. It is still developing, and will be what we wish to have it."

How fortunate that this pent-up reservoir of creative energy, this collective will of a frustrated people, should be expended on revivifying the neglected Holy Land!

The agricultural settlements have played a great part in the training and wholesome adjustment of more than 65,000 teen-age boys and girls who have come to Israel in groups, without their parents.

Not since the Children's Crusade of the Middle Ages has there been such a great influx of boys and girls as the Israel youth immigration, or "Youth Aliyah" as it is called. Aliyah means "to go up" to the land. The first groups to leave the poisoned air of Germany came in 1934. By 1939, some five thousand had arrived, and the rest followed as fast as visas and transportation were provided. After the State of Israel was proclaimed, the children came from the lands of the Middle East and the northern coast of Africa as well as from Europe. For many years, the person behind the steering wheel for this unique adventure in social service was Miss Henrietta Szold, a great humanitarian who had left her home in America to devote herself unceasingly to health activities and social welfare work in Israel.

Whenever possible, the boys and girls were given some training in youth centers, set up in Europe, before the trip across the Mediterranean to Israel, and their welcome into some agricultural settlement. Each group had a leader, who often wasn't much older than the youths. The older pioneers acted as their big brothers and big sisters and introduced them to the new life. For two years each little group remained intact, working in fields, kitchen, laundry, barns, and poultry sheds in the morning, and studying Hebrew and other subjects in the afternoons.

Then came the time for each boy and girl to decide about the future. They could go to a town or city if they wished, but more than ninety percent chose life on the soil. Most often, they would start a new little working community, frequently joining with other groups of congenial young people from different backgrounds.

Gan Shmuel, near the town of Hedera, in the Sharon Plain, is typical of the settlements which have been operating successfully for twenty or thirty years:

The shadows are lengthening. Day is done. The workers have returned from the fields and the citrus groves. The cows are being milked in the barns; the roosters are doing their last crowing for the day; and the children are having their supper.

In the reading room, the radio is bringing in the news of the day. The bookcases and newspaper racks, as well as the tables and chairs, are simple but have a modern touch. A large map of the world adorns the wall.

As the young people come in for a look at the day's paper before supper, they are freshly washed and dressed after the day's toil. They are an intelligent and friendly group in Gan Shmuel. Their faces have satisfied expressions.

In Gan Shmuel there are trees and flowers and shrubbery, and even a carefully nursed grass plot. Some of the wooden shacks and small white concrete houses are vine-covered. In a well-built and spotless barn are cows that might take prizes in an agricultural show. Farther down the road, the chickens are kept in rows of long white houses. The bee-hives fill a field, housed in white boxes. A large structure contains the tractors, the combine, the trucks, and the other machines. A high white tower is used for storing and grinding grain. Close by are acres of green vegetable fields and waving grain, and more acres of orange and grapefruit groves.

The group consisted of forty members when the Jewish National Fund handed over the ground to it in 1920. They were able to absorb sixty more in 1933, and to train various groups of boys and girls who had fled to Palestine from Germany and Nazi-occupied lands during the Hitler regime. Now they are a settlement of over five hundred men, women, and children, and are helping to introduce successive groups of displaced persons to wholesome living and productive work.

In the beginning, lack of funds for water installation and irrigation slowed their progress. Now, as they devote more and more of their land to intensive farming, their income grows.

Not all the Jewish farmers in Israel live in communal settlements. Many thousands own their homes and orange groves and fields. In over a hundred villages, the farmer owns the land, but the large farm machines, the storage sheds, and the dairies are owned cooperatively.

Experience has shown that mixed farming works out best for the small cultivator. Part of his land may be used as an orange grove, part planted with vegetables and fodder crops. A cow provides his family with milk and the remainder of the milk brings in a nice addition to his income. A few hundred white leghorn chickens that are good egg-layers have proved a profitable investment in many places. Orchards and vineyards give variety to the family diet. The independent farmers have been through difficult times in Israel as they have in many other lands. They and their wives have had to work very hard.

Many a new settler, who came with a little capital, built himself a house and planted an orange grove which he thought would yield him a steady income after the five to seven years it takes for citrus trees to reach full fruit-bearing capacity. In 1938-39, citrus exports totaled 15,000,000 cases. Then along came World War II, and for the next six or seven years it was impossible to procure ships for the export of the citrus crop, so thousands of orange and grapefruit growers suffered great financial loss and had to turn to other means for securing a livelihood. Now the citrus growers are experiencing better times. The Israel Citrus Marketing Board represents all growers who are members of various cooperative associations, and it arranges for advertising, sales, and shipments abroad. High quality standards are maintained, and attention is given to proper sorting, packing, and special treatment to prevent rotting.

The kibbutzim are primarily for young people who find it easy to make adjustments or who like living in a large group, with meals served in a large dining hall filled with hundreds of workers. Group existence is especially attractive for those who come to the land without any money for it affords security and a place for themselves on an equal footing with their neighbors.

The middle-aged immigrants who were accustomed to a home filled with their own possessions, who preferred eating meals with just their own family, who wished to continue to exercise private initiative, without having plans discussed and voted upon by a group—have built up the thriving rural villages and towns in Israel or have settled in cities and developed the country's industries and commercial enterprises.

In Israel, there is no telling the background of a farmer. He may once have been a judge or lawyer, a doctor or a scholar. There is one little village that was started entirely by uprooted German physicians who found the land over-supplied with doctors. They specialize in poultry raising and earn their livelihood by sending eggs to markets in Tel Aviv. And they enjoy the peaceful serenity of country life, though it is completely different from anything they had been accustomed to.

The farmer's home is usually a bungalow of white-washed cement, surrounded by a little flower garden. Books, a radio, and a modern bathroom are part of the standard equipment. The houses are equipped with electricity as they have all been constructed in the last couple of decades.

Every village has its kindergarten, school, and synagogue. Most have a cooperative store as well as privately-owned shops, cafés, and cinemas. The residents elect a mayor and village council, and serve on committees so they all have a hand in local developments.

Most of the residents of these villages where property is privately owned are members of the Histadrut, the Federation of Labor, along with the workers in communal agricultural settlements and wage-earners in factories and shops and offices. Payment of dues entitles members to free medical care, hospitalization in every emergency, including child-bearing, and insurance for unemployment and old-age. The Federation has eighteen hundred doctors and nurses on its staff who operate in clinics, dispensaries, stations, convalescent homes, and hospitals. It maintains labor exchanges, a Disablement Fund, and a Widow's and Orphan's Fund.

Hadassah, the Women's Zionist Organization of America, with a membership of 300,000 in the United States, has been active since its founding in 1912 by Miss Henrietta Szold, in helping to provide nurses and doctors, clinics and hospitals, and in introducing progressive health methods such as school lunches and health inspections. It has also taken an active part in the Youth Immigration, vocational training, and the establishment of the Hebrew University-Hadassah Medical School. Other groups of women are active in the Magen David Adom (Red Shield of David), corresponding to the Red Cross, and in helping the new settlers become adjusted to life in their new environment.

The revival of Hebrew as a spoken language was another very difficult and yet basic task of the builders of a Jewish National Home. When the pioneers came to Palestine, they decided that the ancient beautiful Hebrew, the language of the psalmists, prophets, and great law-givers, was their national language and would prove a cohesive influence in the making of a unified nation out of immigrants from dozens of different lands.

Hebrew had remained a language of prayer and study for the Jews all through the centuries, but only during the latter part of the nineteenth century had a movement started toward using it as a spoken language. It had become so much associated with sacred writings that some pious persons objected to its use for ordinary purposes. Many Jews had mixed a few Hebrew words into the language of the country in which they lived. The combination or jargon "Yiddish" originated in Germany in the Middle Ages. "Ladino"—a Spanish mixture, was spread by the refugees from the Spanish Inquisition.

Though many people said it was too much to expect adults as

well as children to learn a difficult new language at the same time that so many other adjustments had to be made, the pioneers went ahead with determination. They would learn it. No matter if the ancient tongue had no terms for automobile, carburetor, football, radio, and thousands of modern inventions and technical terms. These could be developed. Eliezer Ben Yehuda devoted his life to writing a new Hebrew dictionary of twelve volumes. Others followed in his footsteps and worked out medical, technical, and scientific terms. Committees were established to develop the language and to decide on matters of pronunciation, spelling, and syntax. Some English words, like *sport, garage, autobus,* and *America,* were taken into the language without change.

The workers in the agricultural settlements voted that only Hebrew should be spoken. "Speak Hebrew," new settlers were urged by placards in buses and shops. Evening classes for adults were started, and they were attended by grandparents as well as mothers and fathers. The language of instruction in Jewish schools in Palestine had previously varied with the source of their support. Some were conducted in English or French, some in German or Yiddish. The new spirit insisted that Hebrew should be the language used. The seemingly impossible has happened. In one generation Hebrew has become a living national language, used in the streets and at home, in schools and colleges. Newspapers and theatres use Hebrew. It is the official language of the State of Israel.

There is one Hebrew word in constant use. It is *Shalom,* meaning "peace." It is used as a greeting, just as Americans or Englishmen would say "Good Morning" or "Good Evening." The same word serves both occasions. When you see a friend on the street in Israel, you say "Shalom" instead of "Hello." When you say "Goodbye," you repeat again "Shalom." This concentration on the idea of Peace translates into everyday life a basic longing of the people. When glasses are raised, the toast is always *L'Chaim,* meaning "Here's to life."

Today when Leah and Joseph walk home from school along the

palm bordered roads of the pretty village of Pardess Hanna, it seems perfectly natural to them to speak Hebrew.

"Of course, why not?" they would say if questioned. "It is the language of the people of Israel and this is the Land of Israel."

In school they studied about the kings of Israel in their history lesson. They recited by heart some of the warnings of Jeremiah. In their botany class, they discussed how many of the flowers mentioned in the Bible are found in the fields today. In their cooking class, the teacher of course spoke Hebrew when she showed them how to make a fluffy omelet. When they were running races in the school yard during recess, the starter said: *"Ahat, Shtei-im, Shalosh"* for "One, Two, Three."

When they get home, they call "Shalom" to their mother. Joseph puts on his khaki scout uniform, for there is a meeting of the scout troup this afternoon, and Leah reminds him to come home in plenty of time to hear the radio play on the Children's Hour. The possibility that the scout meeting or the radio program will be in any language other than Hebrew does not occur to them.

It is fortunate that modern Hebrew has become firmly established, for now every newcomer knows that he must make an effort to learn it as part of his adjustment. Hebrew becomes the medium through which Jews from China, India, North Africa, Yemen, and Iraq become acquainted with their cousins from Rumania, Bulgaria, Germany, Russia, Poland, England, and the United States, to mention only a few of the seventy lands of origin. Once in Israel, the people mix together. The older settlers constitute a huge reception committee to welcome the new ones— at the dock when they arrive, on the streets, and in the buses. There are people from a dozen countries in every town, every rural settlement, even every large apartment house. There is no doubt that the children born of intermarriages among these people will be just as fine-looking, healthy, and enthusiastic boys and girls as the offspring of an earlier generation.

Personal names have often been adapted to prevailing styles in

various countries. In Israel, there is a tendency to have both first
and last names take on an Hebraic character. There is a new
popularity for such Biblical names as Yaacov (Jacob), Moshé
(Moses), Yitzhak (Isaac), Yosef (Joseph), Eliahu, Eliezar, Shlomo
(Solomon), and Sara, Rachel, Ruth, Naomi, Hanna, Yael, and
Judith.

A prosaic thing like a date may get a little complicated in Israel.
Jews, Christians, and Moslems have different ways of reckoning
the year. The Jews count from their conception of the creation
of the world. The Christian Era dates from the birth of Jesus.
The year 1950 is reckoned as 5710 on the Hebrew calendar. The
Moslems begin from the *Hegira* or flight of Mohammed from
Mecca to Medina in 622, which makes 1328 correspond to the
Christian year 1950.

The Hebrew New Year's Day occurs on the 1st of the Hebrew
month of Tishri, which corresponds to September or October.
The new moon marks the beginning of every month in the
Hebrew year, so each month has twenty-eight or twenty-nine days.
An extra month, instead of an extra day, marks the Hebrew leap
year. Christians are accustomed to having Easter arrive at a
slightly different time each year, and something similar happens
to Jewish holydays. There are only 354 days in the Arab calendar
instead of 365, so their first month, Moharrem, occurs eleven days
earlier each year. Arabs, too, look for the new moon as a sign of
the new month.

The Moslems revere Friday, the Jews hold Saturday as the day
of rest, and the Christians refrain from work on Sunday. Saturday
in Israel has a very special Sabbath atmosphere. To Jews, the new
day begins at sunset, so Friday evening is just as much a part of
the Jewish sabbath as Saturday. Shops are closed early on Fridays
to enable clerks and owners to get home, for the buses stop running before the sun sinks below the horizon. Stores, banks, offices,
cafés, and cinemas remain closed on the Sabbath. The Sabbath is
a time for synagogue attendance and family reunions around the

dinner table, for hiking or visiting friends. Again you hear the word "Shalom" on all sides. On this day the greeting is *"Shabat Shalom"*—"Sabbath Peace."

Don't imagine that it is an easy matter to go into a store and buy half a dozen oranges or a pound of candy. Fruit and candy, as well as vegetables and other foods are sold by the kilogram. A kilo weighs a little less than two pounds. Cloth is measured by the *pic,* which equals sixty-seven centimeters or twenty-seven inches. If you ask a man how much land he owns, he will tell you twenty *dunums,* forty dunums, or as the case may be. A dunum is one quarter of an acre. The metric system is used for weights and measures. The unit of currency is the Israel Pound (I£) divided into 1,000 pruta. Coins of value are 1, 5, 10, 25, 50, 100, and 250 pruta. Banknotes in circulation are for 500 pruta, I£1, I£5, I£10, and I£50.

Earning a living in a new land is a problem that confronts every settler in Israel. Tilling the soil appeals to only one person out of every four in Israel, as it does in the U.S.A. Seventy-five percent of the population prefer to live in towns and cities.

One man looked the country over and found that there was no real expert in the art of grinding sharp edges on steel implements. He went back to Vienna, took a practical course, and became an apprentice for three years. Then he returned to Tel Aviv and set up shop. He puts the edge on the blades of surgical instruments used in hospitals. He gives new life to dull meat-choppers and tools.

Another man developed a good market for enamel signs and posters. As new towns and cities grew, they needed street name-plates and house numbers. Automobiles needed number plates. Some specialized in making candy, others macaroni. Many made use of their hobbies. A former lawyer opened a riding school. A Viennese lady started classes for the making of petit-point embroidery. An artist became a lamp-shade maker.

Today there are many thousand factories and workshops in Israel, employing over 125,000 persons. Practically all the industries had small beginnings, and even now only a few operate on a mass production basis. Until 1917, soap-making and wine production were Palestine's only industries.

It is interesting to note what new initiative has been able to do with the olive oil produced in large quantities locally. Since the days of Cleopatra, olive oil has had a unique reputation for its nourishing and soothing effect on the skin. In Israel it was first marketed as a sunburn lotion. Then it was found possible to make an olive oil cream, so face creams were produced. A shaving stick proved popular because the olive oil produced a fine lather and left the skin soft and supple. After experimenting for two years, an olive oil toothpaste was manufactured. Olive oil soaps, soapflakes, and shampoos meet other needs. These developments were first made in the laboratories of the Palestine Oil Industry, Shemen Ltd., a firm which opened a small plant in the outskirts of Haifa in 1923 for the production of a laundry soap and an inexpensive toilet soap. The following year a department for edible oils was set up, and for the first time olive oil was refined in Palestine. From the beginning the company set itself the highest standards and used modern equipment and the newest methods. Each year has seen a steady plant expansion and it now represents an investment of over a million dollars, and employees number five hundred.

There are numerous textile factories in Israel. Some produce materials for upholstery, curtains, cushions, and bedspreads, others make fabrics for men's shirts and suits and women's dresses. Some plants specialize in canvas for tents. During the war, the output of knit-goods, including underwear, socks, stockings and sweaters increased to five times the amount previously produced. Processes start at spinning and weaving, and go all the way through dyeing and printing to the manufacture of garments—in cotton, rayon, wool, silk, and nylon. A new million-dollar textile mill has just been set up by the Ata Textile Company, Ltd., one of the largest and best operated firms in this field.

Within the framework of the austerity plan introduced by the Government to bring down living costs, local factories are engaged in the manufacture of austerity clothing, shoes, linen goods and furniture.

Men formerly connected with leading pharmaceutical firms in Europe have transferred their activities to Israel, with the result that there are now being produced 800 branded preparations and several hundred non-branded products.

The cutting and polishing of diamonds in Israel gained impetus with the German occupation, during World War II, of Belgium and Holland, former centers of this industry. Within six years, thirty-five plants, with a working force of four thousand persons, had been established. Raw diamonds come from nearby South Africa and the United States takes most of the finished gems.

Most electric appliances are now manufactured or assembled in Israel, including wires, bulbs, lamps, plates, stoves, irons, fans, radios, refrigerators, washing machines, and sewing machines. Cars, trucks, and buses are also assembled locally. All but a small part of the production of Kaiser-Frazer of Israel, Ltd., which started assembling cars in 1951, has been exported, mainly to Turkey, Finland, Norway, Sweden, Iceland, and France.

The skill and know-how of workers and foremen have increased through training and steady employment. The Israel Institute of Technology in Haifa has graduated thousands of engineers and technical workers. There are over twenty-five trade schools, and many economic, industrial, agricultural, and scientific research institutes. The Government Ministry of Trade, Industry and Supply has set up an Industrial Research Department.

The Histadrut, the General Federation of Labor, takes a very active part in promoting industry as well as insuring high wages and the welfare of the workers. In the early days, stone was needed for building purposes, so the Histadrut formed a subsidiary company to buy stone quarries, sometimes in partnership with the Arabs. A million dollars was invested in stone and lime production.

Roads and houses and harbors had to be constructed. The Histadrut organized its own construction and contracting firms, and it made sure its workers were the best in the country. A workers' bank and a workers' insurance company were established, and a central cooperative for housing development provided loans to workers.

When World War II came along, the task of building many army camps, airfields, and military roads, was assigned to the Histadrut's contracting agency, Solel Boneh. The profits from these jobs accumulated, and enabled the Labor Federation to participate actively in expanding the industry of the country. Profits remained large because its officials, even the top chief executives, receive payment according to need and not according to their position or ability. The man who drives a car for the general manger gets more salary from the Histadrut than the general manager, because he has a dependent wife and three small children, while the wife of the manager also works. The woman who scrubs the office floor of the organizer of Arab workers receives more pay than the organizer, because she happens to be a widow with a number of small children.

Industries operated by Solel Boneh or jointly with others, include glass, iron, steel, silicate bricks, cement, tiles, pipes, ceramics, machinery, rubber products and metal goods. The Histadrut publishes newspapers and magazines. It runs airplane and bus lines and takes a part in the creation of an Israel merchant fleet. It owns theatres. hotels, and restaurants. Histadrut finds that it is able to set the standard of wages and working conditions in its own enterprises, and that these standards are so generally accepted by private industry that strikes are seldom called. Some of the Histadrut enterprises are cooperatively owned by the workers, who run the buses, get out the newspapers, and operate the machines in the factories.

Over 500 new enterprises, representing local and foreign investments of more than $200,000,000, have begun operation during the last few years. This fresh capital has been used especially in expanding chemical and metal industries, in the manufacture of machinery, automobile tires and other rubber products, textiles, paper, plastics, clothing and footwear, in the processing of foodstuffs, and in the building of hotels.

The largest chemical firm, Fertilizers and Chemicals, Ltd. of Haifa, manufactures enough superphosphates for fertilizers and sulphuric acid for industrial purposes to make Israel self-sufficient in these important commodities. This firm, in which I£19,000,000 has been invested, produces other basic chemicals also, and its export volume grows from year to year.

Since 1954, all of Israel's newspapers use locally manufactured newsprint. The American-Israel Paper Mills supply the country with bond, kraft, and wrapping paper.

Government aid has been extended to industrial development by way of long-term loans as well as by investment in the development of electricity, mines, and quarries. Over ninety percent of the industrial enterprises in Israel, employing eighty percent of the industrial workers, is privately owned, the remainder being owned by cooperative organizations.

Israel is demonstrating that there need be no sharp dividing line between capitalism and socialism, between free enterprise, communal settlement, and cooperatives. All are patterns of living to suit varying circumstances, and all are today functioning successfully without antagonism within Israel's narrow borders. All are based on freedom for the individual, on the dignity of labor, and on democracy as a working principle.

CHAPTER SIX

Prosperity and Progress

ⅬⅬⅬⅬⅬⅬⅬⅬⅬⅬⅬⅬⅬⅬⅬⅬⅬⅬⅬⅬⅼ

You CAN feel that Haifa is a new progressive town the moment you walk down the gangway from the ship to the broad wharves. In the port area are modern warehouses, and close by is Kingsway, a spacious thoroughfare, wide enough for car parks in the middle of the street. On either side rise white, streamlined office buildings, with shops on the street level.

No use to search for picturesque huts and hovels of an over-crowded Oriental port slum. Haifa's town-planners have guarded its waterfront carefully since the time it was only a small fishing village forty years ago. The old market square and some of the small shops in the north end of the city are the only reminders of the past.

More than one tourist, as he watched the busy throngs of people hurrying to the railroad station, on their way to shops and offices, turning into the Post Office, or standing in queues for buses, has exclaimed in bewilderment: "I thought I was coming to the ancient Holy Land, but all this looks like the most modern of cities!" Few places of its size in the United States have so up-to-date an appearance as Haifa's New Business Center, with its banks, and shops, its cafés, restaurants, and taxi-stands.

The City's main residential suburbs are on the slopes of the Carmel, and one of these suburbs, Hadar Hacarmel (Pride of the

Carmel), with 50,000 inhabitants, has established its own shopping center on Herzl Street.

Here are two of Haifa's finest buildings from an architectural viewpoint—the Law Courts and the Municipal Offices. Americans would call them the Courthouse and the City Hall. Here too is the Israel Institute of Technology, which comprises a Technical College and High School, and a Nautical College. The building that perhaps expresses most clearly Haifa's go-ahead attitude is its Market Building. Erected at a cost of $275,000, it provides hygienic and comfortable accommodation for wholesale and retail trading in perishable foodstuffs, and its five-story building includes an exhibition hall, a restaurant, storage rooms, and an immense public garage.

For those who enjoy walking, the Carmel ridge presents something of a paradise. Its reforestation has kept pace with the building of thousands of attractive homes, surrounded with colorful gardens, and hundreds of apartment houses, with their balconies facing the sea. Half of Haifa comes up to the shady pine forests of the Carmel on Shabat (the Sabbath-day), to enjoy the view and to inspect the rapid building developments on the Central and Western Carmel. For the horseback rider, there are mountain trails leading down to the valleys of the Sharon and the Emek. The boy and girl scouts make good use of these hills and dales for hikes and camping trips.

The fresh sea breezes, the pine-laden air, and the peace and beauty of the surroundings make Mt. Carmel an ideal vacation and health resort, just as the early pioneers had forecast. Its hotels, pensions, and sanitoriums are well patronized by residents of Israel and by visitors from many lands.

Not everyone wants to walk, rest, or recuperate on the Carmel. The most popular form of amusement is furnished by delightful little open-air cafés, where you can listen to good music and dance under the stars in gardens of fig trees and evergreens on a good dance floor. For those who prefer music and dancing accompanied by the lap of waves and sea breezes, there is the Bat Galim Casino, where dance specialties are featured on a night-club program.

Mt. Carmel residents, as well as those living in the Hadar Hacarmel area, have formed associations for the advancement of the interests of their little communities, and special events are scheduled throughout the year, such as art exhibitions, fashion shows, children's festivals, garden-parties, even dog-shows and glider contests, and of course all sorts of concerts.

One of these events was a dramatic presentation of the Book of Ruth, given with all the simplicity and charm of a folk theatre. A hillside provided the natural setting and also a place for five hundred spectators. A full moon cast a magic spell over the whole neighborhood, but spotlights were used with spectacular effect on different parts of the hillside for the various scenes. An inter-locutor read the original of the Biblical story from a large scroll and the Haifa Symphony Orchestra rendered accompanying music especially composed for the occasion.

To see Ruth and Orpah walking down the slope with Naomi and her donkey until they stopped under an olive tree, and Ruth spoke the famous lines: "Entreat me not to leave thee," made one wonder how an indoor stage could ever lend reality to the scene. The spotlight shone on the local maidens presenting a harvest dance, and Boaz first appeared on a handsome Arab steed that, incidentally, took advantage of the sheaves of wheat at hand to do a little nibbling.

The new factories in the Haifa Bay area are not as picturesque as ruined castles, but they can be just as exciting when you con-sider that each plant is helping to build up the economy of the country by producing something needed and at the same time increasing employment. Here the industrial pioneer has staked his faith and his capital in the future of Israel.

This area has had the benefit of exceptional advance planning. The wilderness of thorns and malaria swamps, stretching between Haifa and Acre, was divided up. A large belt of land adjacent to the oil zone, with its great refineries and storage tanks, and close by the airport and the railway terminus, was reserved for industrial development. Large workers' residential suburbs were developed in outlying districts. Water resources were opened up by regulating the flow of the Kishon River into well-designed channels. A large power station was erected to supply industrial needs. Already over a hundred factories are in operation.

The first housing scheme was launched in 1932. At present the residential zone holds a population of 50,000 persons, residing in small one-family white-washed concrete houses. Government lands have been allotted for veterans' housing schemes. An agricultural zone is devoted to vegetable gardening and fruit-growing.

Ocean liners and cargo ships can now bring passengers and freight to the quayside in Haifa Port, as the harbor has been dredged and deepened. Added port facilities have been made available at the mouth of the nearby Kishon River. New equipment and warehouses have also been added to the ports of Tel Aviv and Jaffa, where ships must still anchor off shore and the cargo be transferred to small lighters.

The Haifa airfield is used by Cyprus Airways and local planes. The Lydda Airport, home base of Israel's airline, El Al, is much larger and is a scheduled stop on ten international airlines.

Haifa is a central point in northern Israel from which dozens of side trips to points of interest may be made, but no tourist or new settler is long content to be in Israel without following the trail of countless pilgrims to the Holy City of Jerusalem.

The railways are under Government operation, and the trend toward motor travel has not encouraged huge expenditures for modern railroad equipment. All important centers of population are connected by good, all-weather roads, and links to new settlements have been constructed. As few people possess their own cars, the use of buses and taxis has become widespread. In order to make the maximum use of cars, individual seats are sold, and the shared taxis operate on regular schedules between the cities.

If you drive along the coastal road which leads south from Haifa through the Sharon Plain to join the main highway that connects

Tel Aviv with Jerusalem, you climb upwards toward the end of the journey, past the crumbling terraces of the barren Mountains of Judea, and first glimpse the Holy City silhouetted across the crest of the range.

Before Palestine was partitioned, you could proceed eastwards, across the fertile Emek, the Valley of Esdraelon, with its fields laid out with checkerboard neatness, and follow along the old inland caravan route, now outside the borders of Israel, past Jenin and Nablus, to the top of a high plateau.

On this route, as you approached Jerusalem from the Nablus Road, you came toward a vista of towers, minarets, domes, and flat roofs at different levels—surrounded by the picturesque walls of the Old City rising above deep ravines, while the new city outside the walls stretched far to the south and west.

To behold Jerusalem for the first time is a unique experience. The spirit of the past seems to hover over its masses of rose-tinted marble and stone. More than any other place in the world, it has been mystically enshrined in the hearts of millions down through the ages. You are on your way back to forgotten centuries, and the modern homes, churches, and hospitals that you pass by in the outlying sections have only a secondary interest.

One entrance to the Old City is the great Damascus Gate, the most beautiful of the eight gates that form part of the contour of the ancient wall—the wall breached a dozen times by invading armies and rebuilt by Saladin in the twelfth century, and again by Suleiman the Magnificent in the sixteenth century.

Broad marble steps lead down to the bewildering array of Oriental sights and smells in suks and bazaars, and to the closely packed collection of tombs and temples, monuments and monasteries. The Old City is really a great museum of three thousand years of history, still throbbing with life and color.

Donkeys and camels can navigate up and down the stepped alleys which serve as street, pavement, and buying arcade, but here the honk-honk of the motor car is never heard. As you watch the milling throng of village Arabs in their striped gabardines and colorful girdles and turbans against the background of tiny booths filled with assorted merchandise and fruit, you feel that you have wandered into a scene of a stage. Suddenly you in your modern clothes seem as out-of-place as the Yankee at King Arthur's Court.

Inside the Gate, you pause to wonder at the labyrinth of houses and courtyards that have meant home, generation after generation, to families who have never heard of Moving Day. Some of these dwellings are built right into the city wall today as in Bible times. You may discover the steps which permit you to scale the walls and imagine yourself a sentry standing guard almost a thousand years ago, when the Crusaders occupied the town. The walls rise to an average height of thirty-eight feet and contain thirty-four towers as they form an irregular quadrangle two and a half miles in circumference.

If you stand about with an inquiring attitude that marks you as a tourist, it will not be long before a guide will spot you and come forward to suggest:

"You want to see the Church of the Holy Sepulchre? Come with me."

You follow and soon, after many turnings, you descend the steps to the courtyard of the great edifice which marks the most sacred spot in all Christendom. This church, with its conspicuous dome, surmounted by a gilded cross, occupies a site revered for centuries as Golgotha, the Hill of Calvary. Historians record how the Empress Helena, mother of Constantine—the first Roman emperor to adopt Christianity, made a pilgrimage to Jerusalem in the fourth century and here discovered the tomb of Christ. Church after church was erected over this spot, only to be destroyed in successive attacks on Jerusalem. The Church received its present form from the Crusaders, but it has been demolished and rebuilt several times since then.

In the center of the rotunda is the Holy Sepulchre. The church is shared by six denominations, and each has its appointed chapels and rights. Forty-eight perpetually burning lamps, belonging to different churches, keep watch over the marble-covered tomb. It is from this spot that the "Miracle of the Holy Fire" occurs during the Greek Orthodox celebration of Easter, witnessed always by huge throngs.

From the Church of the Holy Sepulchre, you may follow the Via Dolorosa, the narrow winding street along which Jesus carried the cross as he proceeded from the court of Pontius Pilate. The traditional site of the Prætorium, or Judgment Hall, is now occupied by a Moslem school. The original steps of this building were transported to Rome, where they are known as the Scala Santa. Close by is the Church of St. Anne, a fine example of a Crusader Abbey. Tradition holds this as the site of the home of the parents of the Virgin and the birthplace of Mary.

To the many churches, monasteries, and convents in the Old City, many edifices have been added in recent years in the newer sections. Outstanding in architectural beauty are the Anglican Cathedral of St. George, the Scottish Church of St. Andrew, the Russian many-domed cathedral, and the Franciscan Church of All Nations in the Garden of Gethsemane.

Another day you will want to enter the Old City through the Jaffa Gate and explore the ancient Citadel with its famous Tower of David, its beautiful façades and turrets, and its moss-grown empty moat, dating from the time of King Herod. You will visit the Haram al Sherif, the former Temple Area, now a walled enclosure held by the Moslems as their sacred shrine. It contains the famous octagonal mosque, the Dome of the Rock, sometimes erroneously called the Mosque of Omar, in the center of a marble platform reached by eight different flights of steps leading from the courtyard. The lower half of the building is paneled with white marble slabs, and the upper half is covered with bluish-green tiles, inscribed with quotations from the Koran.

In the center of the mosque is a rock of many traditions, known as the Foundation Stone of the World. On this rock it is said the patriarch Abraham was ready to sacrifice his son Isaac. Here the Temple altar stood. The Moslems hold that it was from this rock that Mohammed ascended to heaven on the back of his winged steed, and they point out the footprint of a horse. The Crusaders worshipped here when they converted the Mosque into the Templum Domini for Christian use.

Both the Dome of the Rock and the adjoining Mosque of Aksa —also a very beautiful structure—were built in the seventh century by Caliph Abd el-Malik when he wished to raise the prestige of Jerusalem as a holy city of Islam in competition with Mecca and Medina, two holy cities of the Moslems which were held by rivals for Islamic power.

From the Mosque of Aksa, a wide staircase leads down to Solomon's Stables—a vast array of pillared and vaulted avenues. In this subterranean crypt are eighty-eight massive square pillars arranged in fifteen rows. The Crusaders, like Solomon, used the vaults as stables, and the small holes drilled in the angles of the pillars show where the Knights Templars and the Kings of Jerusalem in the twelfth century chained their chargers.

For the Jews, the place in the Old City of greatest historical and emotional significance is the Western Wall, sometimes called the "Wailing Wall"—the sole remaining fragment of the Temple, which was set on fire by the Roman soldiers of Titus in the year 70 A.D. Here pious Jews wended their way on sabbaths and festivals.

Until recently, on the ninth of the Hebrew month of Ab, which occurs during August, many thousands made a pilgrimage to this spot, for it was on this date that the destruction of both the first and the second Temples took place. Beginning at sundown, there was an unending line of men and women, boys and girls, filing silently through the narrow lanes to stand before those ancient stones. As night came on, the fitful glare of torches disclosed the figure of many an old, white-bearded man in a fur-trimmed turban of black velvet, with a striped prayer-shawl over his shoulders, reaffirming his faith—a striking scene worthy of poet and artist.

In the lower part of the sixty-foot Temple wall are several rows of great stone blocks, from the days of King Herod in the first century, in an excellent state of preservation. The plants between the stones are sometimes identified as "the hyssop which springeth out of the wall."

Few Christians who come to Jerusalem for religious inspiration fail to journey five miles southward to the little Town of Bethlehem, nestling among the Judean Mountains 2500 feet above sea level. The most sacred shrine of this many spired town is the Church of the Nativity, built by the Emperor Constantine in the year 330 A.D., the oldest church still in use. A flight of stairs at the eastern end of the church leads to a cave or grotto, lined with silken tapestries and decorated with dozens of antique hanging lamps of silver. A large bronze star embedded in the flooring marks the traditional birthplace of Jesus. To worship here on Christmas Eve comes a continuous stream of pilgrims from every corner of the world, tiny candles in hand to light up the dim interior.

Outside the old Crusader Wall of the Greek Orthodox Monastery, underneath the stars, members of the Western Christian communities gather to sing the familiar tunes of "Silent Night, Holy Night" and "Hark the Herald Angels Sing," while the chimes and bells of Bethlehem, transmitted by radio, echo round the world.

Shortly before midnight, the Latin Church on the north side of the Church of the Nativity fills up with people of all nationalities and, as mass begins, the Latin Patriarch, in his Pontifical vestments, carries a small statue of the Christ-child, made many years ago in Spain, to the Manger, where it remains until Epiphany, on the sixth of January.

The new districts of Jerusalem now contain many of the features of a modern metropolis—modern homes, hotels, and shops, and yet the Eternal City is subtly different from other cities.

In New York or San Francisco, the new immigrant soon learns to put aside his old customs, and he tries to look and act as much as possible like his neighbors. But in Jerusalem, the settlers from fifty countries feel that they may live and dress according to the very latest ideas and styles or the most ancient.

If you ride in early-morning buses, you will see boys and girls on their way to school who look very much like Tom and Mary in Maine and Georgia, only they will be chattering away in Hebrew more likely than in English. Clerks and lawyers with their briefcases will be hurrying to their offices, along with shopowners who will soon be rolling up the heavy iron Venetian blinds or shutters that protect the shop fronts during the night.

Among the thousands of university students, including some from the United States and other countries, proceeding to classrooms and laboratories, will be prospective teachers, nurses, doctors, dentists, pharmacists, social workers, and nuclear research scientists, who are working on the exploitation of uranium from Israel's vast supply of phosphate rock and the application of atomic energy to many constructive uses.

Young people with artistic talents will be heading for the Bezalel School of Arts and Crafts, which has already produced many skillful workers in silver, copper, wood, ceramics, handwoven textiles, and rugs.

Tourists from every part of the world may be seen, as well as delegates who have come to attend some international conference, convention, or exposition. You may catch sight of Israel's legislators on their way to the Knesset. The bearded rabbis with long black coats, the Yeshiva students with side-curls framing pale faces underneath wide-brimmed black hats, and the Greek Orthodox priests with high-crowned black hats and flowing robes, all seem somehow to fit into the scene.

Later in the morning, the ladies who dressed smartly in Vienna and Berlin, London, and New York, continue to look chic as they go shopping in Jerusalem or stop in at their favorite pastry shop for coffee and cheesecake.

Saturday afternoon is a good time to see the Oriental or Sephardic Jews, who form a considerable part of the population. They or their ancestors have come from Spain, Portugal, and Turkey, from Egypt, Algeria, Morocco, and Tunisia, from Damascus, Baghdad,

Iran, and Yemen. Bokharian, Georgian, and Kurdish Jews have migrated from regions in Asia that lie to the south of Russia. Most of these people live in their own little "quarters" of the widespread city, but towards the end of the Sabbath-day, when the shops are still closed, and no buses and very little traffic on wheels disturbs the peaceful atmosphere, they throng down Herzl Road in a great promenade. Some turn the corner at King David Avenue and mingle with the young and old of the western communities who have been born in Poland and Russia, Rumania and Germany, America and South Africa, who are also out to enjoy a leisurely stroll.

"So many varieties of human beings!" you comment as you walk past the Public Gardens, and pause a moment to watch the glow of the setting sun turn the walls of the Old City a pale gold. "What holds them together? What do they have in common?"

No need to ask this question if you had been in the homes of these people the previous evening and had seen how they ushered in the Sabbath with a common tradition—the white tablecloth, the gleaming sabbath candles, the blessings pronounced over loaves of white bread and a cup of wine, the family dressed in their sabbath clothes gathered around the table for the best meal of the week. With religious convictions, traditions, and home observances all very similar, the outward characteristics acquired in Europe, Asia, or Africa do not prevent a feeling of essential unity.

On a Saturday afternoon you may change the scene like the pages of a picture book. If you turn to the left off King David Avenue, five minutes walk will bring you to the King David Hotel, the Waldorf Astoria of Jerusalem. Here a mixed crowd of smartly dressed men and women will be dancing to the rhythm of a Viennese trio on marble tiles inside the great lounge, or sipping afternoon tea on the terraces overlooking a garden of many hues, with the Old City forming a glamorous backdrop.

Antiquities have never found a lovelier resting place than in the Palestine Archæological Museum, near Herod's Gate, built with funds provided by John D. Rockefeller, Jr. Beauty of line and color find expression in the white marble-domed buildings, in the exquisite niches of glazed tiles, and in the courtyard with its azure pool containing a few delicately colored waterlilies. Its charming gardens made a perfect background for intimate music recitals in the days when Jerusalem was a unified city.

Government House, formerly the residence of high commissioners, set among terraced gardens overlooking the weird contours of the Judean Desert, is another architectural gem. James N. Jarvie of New Jersey gave a million dollars to erect the Y.M.C.A. building, opposite the King David Hotel, as a great international meeting-place for people of all creeds and nationalities. It ranks as one of the most beautiful buildings in the world devoted to communal purposes. The semicircular group of buildings which form the headquarters of the Jewish Agency and the new government buildings are impressive in their simplicity.

These edifices, added to the array of churches, schools, and hospitals, give the city on the hills a stately beauty.

The Hebrew University and Medical Center on Mt. Scopus, though a little removed from the center of town, had been playing an increasingly important role in Jerusalem life until access to them was prevented by the Arab Legion of Jordan. Days of peace will bring the resumption of their former noteworthy activities, now carried on in other parts of the city where safety is assured. The University, open to all without distinction of race or creed, provides opportunities for both undergraduate and graduate study. The staff includes two hundred and fifty professors, lecturers, and research assistants, and the student body numbers over three thousand. University departments include the Humanities, Mathematics and Sciences, Agriculture, Law, Economics and Social Sciences, Medicine, Dentistry, and Pharmacology.

The Jewish National and University Library, one of the first buildings to be erected, contains 600,000 volumes. In its vaults and archives are many priceless ancient manuscripts and one modern one—Albert Einstein's *Essay on the Theory of Relativity*. Books, magazines, and exhibits are sent out on loan to towns and

rural settlements, and during the summer months university professors give extension courses in various parts of the country.

A unique little museum housed a wonderful collection of the
flowers, plants, and even the thorns mentioned in the Bible, preserved in all the beauty of their natural color and form by a
special process.

A Museum of Jewish Antiquities at the University supplements
the excellent collections of the Bezalel Museum in town, and the
archæological collections of the Jewish Palestine Exploration
Society. It contains fine examples of ancient pottery, glass, and
alabaster, and coins of many periods. The Department of Geology
boasts a collection of 500,000 specimens of rocks and minerals.
Texts and gramophone records of various types of Jewish music
are assembled in the Archives of Oriental Music.

The University's open-air theatre was one of the features of the
university most appreciated by residents of Jerusalem. Young
and old came up Mt. Scopus to take their places on the stone steps
in an amphitheatre on the hillside campus for symphony concerts
and dance recitals. No more charming or dramatic stage effects
can be imagined than the colors, lights, and shadows cast by the
setting sun on the bare hills as they drop precipitously toward
the Dead Sea and the Mountains of Moab. The audience faced
this scene, framed in the portals of the amphitheatre platform.

Adjoining the campus are the first buildings of the Medical
School, the Henrietta Szold School of Nursing, and the well-
equipped Hadassah Hospital. As the use of these buildings has
been prevented by the Arabs, a new Hadassah Hospital is being
erected near Ein Karim. Although forced to continue in impro-
vised laboratories and classrooms, the Hebrew University-Hadassah Medical School has rapidly expanded.

In the suburbs to the west of Jerusalem are Mt. Herzl, the final
resting place of Theodor Herzl, and the new Jerusalem Convention Center.

Forty miles separate Jerusalem from Tel Aviv. A short journey in a car will take you from one of the world's oldest cities to

one of the world's newest, from the quiet sedate atmosphere of home-lovers to the gay and flamboyant tempo of young people who are awake and restless until late at night in streets, theatres, and cafés. The difference in atmosphere between the two cities is similar to what you feel in coming to New York after visiting Washington, D. C.

Tel Aviv is the commercial, industrial, and cultural center of the State of Israel. In and around Tel Aviv are most of the country's factories and workshops. Here are located the headquarters of banks, insurance companies, import and export firms, housing and development companies. Hebrew newspapers, magazines and books are printed here in eighty printing plants.

Tel Aviv believes in going forward at a fast pace, ever since the day in 1909 when a group of Jewish residents of the ancient seaport of Jaffa began to build houses on the empty sand dunes to the north. What they thought would be a suburb soon developed into a bustling town with a personality all its own. In 1922, it had 15,000 settlers. By 1932, the number had grown to 45,000. Two or three years later, the population reached the 100,000 mark, and today it is over 200,000.

During the first twenty years of its existence, houses were put up rapidly, torn down, and built again, each time with better architectural style and construction. It is a city of white concrete houses, each with protruding balconies and colorful gardens. Both wood and stone were difficult to obtain, hence the use of concrete. The houses are not single homes but contain numerous small apartments, and more often than not, one room of the small apartment is rented out. There is a striking absence of palatial mansions. People live simply, without any attempt at display.

Tel Aviv is a city of young workers, young writers, artists, musicians,—and young mothers with baby carriages. Israel is, at the moment, a nation of young people. Less than fifteen percent of the population have passed their fiftieth birthday.

These young people knew what they wanted as they built up Tel Aviv. They wanted sunshine and flowers. Hence the broad streets, the gardens, the parks, and the wide, flower-bordered esplanade along the sea-front. They wanted comradeship and laughter, and so they patronize night after night the little sidewalk cafés or join the promenade at the beach. They wanted good music, the theatre and opera, in addition to the latest films. They wanted books and pictures and exhibitions, and, of course, they wanted good schools for their children. And they wanted a harbor.

Today they have all these things, and the satisfaction of creating a new city by their own efforts and self-imposed taxation seems to provide them with an extra measure of buoyancy and vigor, despite the long months of hot, humid days and nights they live through every summer. Perhaps this joy of living is what attracts new settlers and keeps Tel Aviv perpetually bursting at the seams.

Tel Avivians like the theatre, and they have built an imposing edifice, seating fifteen hundred—with air-conditioning and a revolving stage, for the productions of Habimah, the National Theatre. Plays by Shakespeare, Shaw, Racine, Ibsen, Tolstoy, and other writers, are translated into Hebrew and performed before capacity audiences. Many plays by local writers on historical themes are also produced.

Ohel, the Workers' Theatre, another repertoire company, has its own building too. A third company, known as Matate (The Broom) has won a special place for itself, for its shows are always satirical and mirror the daily life roundabout with touches of humor. Performances of a miniature theatre and excellent puppet shows are held from time to time. In Israel, of course, the dolls speak and sing in Hebrew. One "company" is made up of one hundred dolls. The Chamber Theatre is also popular.

Tel Aviv likes the theatre, but it *loves* good music. Most of its mixed population know enough Hebrew to understand Hebrew plays and lectures, but *all* comprehend the international language of melody, and they throng to concerts and recitals and programs of chamber music.

The concerts of the Israel Philharmonic Symphony Orchestra are gala occasions. This orchestra was assembled by the late Bronislaw Hubermann from among Europe's most talented young musicians when the Hitler shadow began to lengthen. Its first performance was given in 1936 under the baton of Arturo Toscanini. Since then many famous musicians have acted as guest conductors and soloists, and the soloists have also included many talented young Israel artists. Packed houses have always greeted the orchestra, even in days of war and tension.

The four theatrical companies, the folk opera, the puppet shows, and the orchestra all give performances regularly in Jerusalem and Haifa as well as in their home city, and occasionally they delight audiences in rural towns and agricultural settlements.

The Tel Aviv Museum, on Rothschild Boulevard, formerly the home of its first mayor, gives local artists an opportunity to show their work to the public and presents special exhibitions from time to time. A new building is soon to be erected on a site made available by the city which will be known as the Artists' and Sculptors' Center. The city's two hundred journalists and authors have a Press Club. The six-story Manufacturers' Association Building on Montifiore Street houses a permanent exhibit of Israeli-made products, and is the scene of Fashion Shows which are held twice a year for foreign buyers.

Most of the factory buildings have been designed to afford the workers light and air. Near-by Ramat Gan has over five hundred factories, and yet it is a garden suburb, with green fields and orange groves surrounding many of the buildings. The distribution of the industrial plants over a wide area enables employees to live in outlying sections rather than crowd into closely packed tenements.

Tel Aviv is sport-minded. Twelve sport organizations keep their members active. The Ramat Gan Stadium, seating 60,000 spectators, is the scene of national championship contests and the World Maccabiah Games. Close by, on the Yarkon River, are facilities for rowing and sailing. The Israel Soccer Team has crossed the ocean a number of times to meet American teams. Football and tennis, swimming and water polo, basketball and hockey are all more popular than baseball.

Tel Aviv's young people wanted a harbor. They wanted it so much that every able-bodied man volunteered to work for a day to help build that harbor. They invested over a million dollars of their hard-earned wages in that port, and they arranged that some of them would perform all the work—porterage, lighterage, stevedoring, and boat building. Thousands of young men were trained as maritime workers, and many of them today are manning the ships of the Israel Merchant Fleet. Jewish youth has turned to life on the sea as well as life on the soil.

As new Jewish immigrants moved into homes in Jaffa vacated by the Arabs as a result of the war in 1948, the municipal services of Tel Aviv were extended to the parent city of Jaffa and in October, 1949, the city of Tel Aviv-Jaffa with a combined population of over 350,000 became an entity.

In addition to cities, Palestine possesses dozens of towns. Like everything else in this land of diversities and contrasts, there is no dull sameness or monotony about these communities. Not one has a pattern of a Main Street with a corner drugstore, a gas station, and half a dozen shops showing nationally advertised brands of merchandise. Each place has its own individuality, its history, and its reasons for existence.

Moslem towns outside the borders of Israel, like Nablus and Hebron—picturesque and colorful, with bazaars full of assorted spices and grains, rolls of cloth, crudely cut sheepskin coats, and clay water-jugs decorated with orange, blue, and black stripes, still retain something of the story-book quality of the Orient. But even here, schools and clinics and trips to near-by cities have opened the doors to new ideas. General prosperity has enabled many residents to build new stone houses, and the boundaries of both Nablus and Hebron are expanding along their mountainsides. The use of modern furniture and dishes is now the rule rather than the exception among Arabs of means who live in towns.

Industrial progress has been slow, due chiefly to the lack of trained technicians and foremen. The Muezzin's melodious call to prayer sounds out five times a day from the high minaret of the town mosque. The cafés are full, no matter what the hour, with men quietly sipping black coffee or inhaling the water-filtered smoke of a nargile, while the clack-clack of the backgammon players is often the only sound that breaks the sleepy atmosphere.

The sweet cakes for which Nablus bakeshops are famous are just as much a treat to the local boys and girls as ice-cream cones—of which they as yet know little. The old Roman bath-houses supply just as satisfying steam rub-downs as any modern Turkish bath establishment. The slow, easy, old-fashioned ways of living and dressing are not to be cast aside too quickly, think these people, until the advantages of Western styles are more manifest.

The central courtyards, into which open all the rooms of the house—very similar to Spanish patios—often contain lovely secret gardens of roses and jasmine, with a well or fountain in the center, shaded by a slender peach tree or a row of tall cypresses. They afford complete privacy for work or relaxation out-of-doors.

Bethlehem and Beit Jallah, Nazareth and Ramallah, are Christian Arab towns—clean and well-ordered, with charming views of hills and dales roundabout. Churchbells and old monastery chimes ring out the hours while the inhabitants go through the day without any modern hurry and bustle. Near-by olive groves, vineyards, and fields of grain and vegetables supply work for most of the men and boys, and the women and girls occupy themselves with household tasks and colorful cross-stitch embroidery. The Christian Arabs, most of whom have a European ancestor in their family genealogy, are among the first to take advantage of today's educational opportunities. In the American Friends' excellent schools in Ramallah many of the students have mothers and fathers who attended these schools in their youth. When you hear an American home economics teacher instruct these modern, wide-awake pretty girls, it is hard to realize that you are in a small Arab town in distant Palestine. But as yet these boys and girls represent only the vanguard of change.

The world comes to Bethlehem in pilgrimage, like the waves

of the sea to a far shore, and the world returns from the famous
manger, leaving the inhabitants of the little mountain town un-
changed as the receding waves the sands they have touched. You
wonder what mysterious force keeps the fine-looking women of
Bethlehem so attached to their high-peaked hats covered with
trailing white veils—a style which they alone have adhered to
since the days of the Crusaders—eight hundred years ago! Perhaps
they have seen so many fashions come and go, as worn by the
visitors from every part of the globe, that it has been difficult to
know which style to prefer. More likely, each daughter has taken
it as a matter of course that she would dress exactly as her mother
has done.

Acre, with its high white minarets and swaying palm trees, with
its sea wall and earthworks, built on Crusader foundations, is one
of the most picturesque towns in Israel. Its chief monument is
the mosque of Jezzar Pasha, built about 1790. The ancient citadel,
once a Crusader fortress containing many old dungeons, has been
recently used as a prison.

Acre was the capital of the Crusader Kingdom in the days of
Richard the Lion-Hearted and was the scene of bitter fighting.
Its riches and splendor grew until it ranked second only to Constantinople as the chief mart between East and West. Successive
bombardments in the course of the centuries destroyed the city
time and again. In 1799, Acre was besieged by Napoleon, but
his forces were obliged to retire, owing to the arrival of the British
fleet. Today it is no longer a seaport, as its inner harbor is choked
with sand. Prior to the construction of the Damascus-Haifa Railway, all the wheat trade from the East passed through Acre in long
caravans. During the season, two or three thousand camels would
arrive daily, laden with grain. You may still visit the walled-in
enclosures, known as caravanserai, but their bustling activity is a
thing of the past.

Most of the Jewish towns are located along the coastal plain.
They started as little farming communities. Petach Tikvah (Gate-
way of Hope), northeast of Tel Aviv, on the main highway to

Haifa, is now a busy municipality of 35,000 inhabitants, with dozens of factories and workshops interspersed among its orange groves. Petach Tikvah was founded back in 1879, and for the first four decades of its existence remained a straggling village, but today its main street is a busy thoroughfare, with shops and garages, beauty parlors and office buildings, a bank or two, and a moving picture theatre. Men, women, and children dress pretty much as they do in American small towns. Most women prefer gay kerchiefs to hats.

Rishon le Zion (First to Zion), also started by the first wave of early pioneers, is another of the towns with industrial plants supplementing the chief activity of agriculture. In this case it is largely viniculture. Rishon le Zion is famous for its wine cellars. Here, in great vaulted caverns, carefully constructed below the grape-pressing rooms, are 105 giant tanks with glazed interiors, each with a capacity of 30,000 quarts. Fifty varieties of wine are produced here and are marketed all over the world. During the vintage season, it is an interesting sight to watch the grapes being brought in by the three hundred growers who are members of the cooperative which runs the plant. In the garden adjoining the wine cellars is a famous Palm Alleé, planted by the first settlers sixty years ago.

Rehovot is a pretty town in the center of the citrus region. Mile after mile of the shiny green leaves stretch in every direction. Situated here are the laboratories, fields, and headquarters of a very progressive Agricultural Experiment Station, as well as the buildings of the Daniel Sieff Institute for Chemical Research and the new Chaim Weizmann Scientific Institute. Meetings, lectures, concerts, and theatrical performances are held in a community auditorium. Dr. Weizmann, the first President of the State of Israel, had his home in Rehovot. The peaceful beauty of the surroundings and the cultural and scientific interests of many of its residents give this town of 25,000 something of the atmosphere of a college town.

CHAPTER SEVEN

Unfinished Drama

A TOUCH of the eternal clings to the bare hills of Israel which have seen a dozen civilizations rise and fall. The drama of the Holy Land will never be finished. A rejuvenated land and an ancient nation—born anew—have set the stage for a fresh approach to the acquisition of those "Four Freedoms" which symbolize the aspirations of mankind.

Again the world looks on, waits, doubts—and finally acclaims —the spirit and the methods with which the people of Israel in the Land of Israel are meeting their latest and perhaps their most severe challenge. This challenge is self-imposed. It is the determination to hold the gates of the land wide open to every Jew who seeks entry.

Fortunate indeed that every challenge to Israel is like a shot in the arm, and that every resident in Israel and many a Jew and non-Jew far beyond its borders reacts:

"I am a member of the generation privileged to witness the rebuilding of the Land of Israel. What share can I have in this wonderful adventure, this dream of the centuries coming true before my very eyes?"

Jews have been pouring into Israel by land, sea, and air in such numbers that new settlements have had to be started, not by dozens but by hundreds. It had been expected that, regardless of an already existing shortage of housing and food, provision would somehow be made for 100,000 newcomers a year, but 680,-000 settlers arrived in Israel's first four years, and since then the immigration has continued, though on a much smaller scale.

Previous *Aliyahs*—or waves of immigration—had consisted of young, healthy pioneers, often carefully selected and trained in advance, or older men with technical experience and some capital. But what now? Ninety-five percent of the present influx have spent long years in the miserable concentration and D.P. camps of Europe; they are fleeing from lands of persecution. Most are destitute, undernourished, poorly clad. They need food, shelter, clothing, medical care, and vocational training, as well as integration into the life of the country. Thousands of the children among them have never known what it means to have a home or to go to a school. They need a wealth of love and understanding care and attention.

So great a challenge has won needed cooperation from many sources. The U.S. Import-Export Bank has made loans to the new state of $135,000,000, and during 1951-54 the U.S. Government voted $192,000,000 to provide Grants-in-Aid and Technical Assistance so that essential supplies could be imported and wisely used.

Large amounts, totaling hundreds of millions, have poured into the funds of the Jewish Agency and as investments in Israel Bond Issues, from Jews in the United States, Canada, South America, South Africa, Great Britain, and other countries, as good-will offerings, as pledges of solidarity with the pioneers in their great undertaking. Thousands of young people in these lands have crossed the oceans to play a part in the actual exciting up-building of the new state.

Private capital has found investment in Israeli enterprises a good business proposition. The large amount already invested in Israel's securities, traded on the Tel Aviv Stock Exchange, is being constantly added to by industrialists and men and women of means in many parts of the world. Thousands of business men, engineers, technicians, scientists, and large-scale housing and building experts, ship-builders, film producers, and manufacturers are making personal trips to this new center of dynamic growth. Private capital is as welcome and as necessary, and as carefully protected, as is the individual who comes with nothing but the will to work and create.

The Israel population is taxing itself heavily to meet all costs of government and the extraordinary expenses attached to having 70,000 men and women in the army during periods of emergency. For the inhabitants of Israel, the expansion of their numbers in such rapid fashion means daily adjustments. It means the more closely packed utilization of every room. The houses vacated by the Arabs have been occupied, whenever possible. Every available tent is bulging. The camps formerly used by the British Army have been turned into reception centers. Efforts are being made to speed up new housing projects, including the use of prefabricated homes. The population has accepted cheerfully an exacting austerity program, with continued rationing of many foods and the exclusion of luxury imports.

One little detail symbolizes the spirit of the welcome the people of Israel are extending to the newcomers. After each immigrant is registered at a reception center, he is provided with a pass for free bus travel so that he may actually see the land that he had dreamed of for so many years, sometimes behind barbed wire; so that he may contact relatives and friends, if he has any; and so that he may make, if possible, his own arrangements for lodging and a job. These thousands of extra bus passengers mean endless standing in line for the regular inhabitants, but they understandingly shrug their shoulders and say *"Ain Davar"*—"It doesn't matter."

Surveys made by American engineers and economists make clear that large-scale irrigation projects can open up new areas and extend the borders of those areas now under intensive cultivation, and that industry and trade can expand to such an extent that

Israel will become the leading producer and merchant of the Middle East. Peaceful uses of atomic energy will speed progress.

The increase in the population will mean larger markets for vegetables, for building stone, cement, and furniture, and for the thousand and one articles which are needed in daily living. Large new markets are in prospect in Europe and England for winter vegetables grown in the semi-tropical Jordan Valley when air transport is available. Fresh citrus and citrus concentrates are being welcomed in vitamin-starved countries.

Industrial plants are being modernized with new machinery, more automatic devices, and the introduction of assembly lines, so that unit costs will be reduced. Imports of additional raw materials will accelerate production in many fields. With a further improvement in packaging, advertising, and salesmanship, Israel cosmetics, drugs, dentifrices, candies, leather goods, ceremonial objects, souvenirs, and gift items will be able to compete on world markets—are already finding a ready sale in many countries.

Modern pilgrimages to the Holy Land by air, sea, and rail will tax transport facilities for many years. The scenic beauty, the fine climate, and the presence of the mineral springs of great therapeutic value at Tiberias, El Hamma, and on the shores of the Dead Sea, together with all the vast array of historical and Biblical landmarks, will attract visitors from far and near.

Airplane travel will make possible short side trips to the enchanting Gulf of Aqaba; to Petra, the flame-tinted Nabataean stronghold, with its marvelously carved stone caves, baths, and amphitheatre; to Jerash, whose Roman-built temples, forum, stadium, and triumphal archway are reminders of past glory; to Kerak, with its wonderful Crusader Castle still towering high above the valley; and to the Cedars of Lebanon, where perfect skiing conditions prevail on the surrounding slopes until late in March.

The nations of the world have a particular interest in Israel's political status. After World War I, the League of Nations acted as arbiter of its destiny, and after World War II, the United Nations Organization assumed the responsibility. Thus Israel is unique in the political sphere just as it is unique religiously and historically.

Along with the rest of the world, what Israel needs most is peace and security. Mistrust, fear, hatred, bombs and bullets seem particularly regrettable in the Holy Land. Both the people of Israel and their Arab neighbors have everything to gain through cooperation and goodwill.

Twenty-seven hundred years ago, the Prophet Isaiah dreamed of a sanctified Jerusalem and the coming of universal peace. His words have echoed down the centuries in the hearts of Israel and all mankind:

> It shall come to pass in the end of days,
> That the mountain of the Lord's house shall be
> Established as the highest mountain,
> And shall be exalted above the hills.
> All the nations shall flow to it,
> And many peoples shall go and say:
> "Come, let us go up to the mountain of the Lord,
> To the house of the God of Jacob,
> That He may teach us of His ways,
> And we will walk in His paths."
> For out of Zion shall go forth the Law,
> And the word of the Lord from Jerusalem.
>
> He shall judge between the nations,
> And shall decide for many peoples;
> And they shall beat their swords into plowshares,
> And their spears into pruning hooks;
> Nation shall not lift up sword against nation,
> Neither shall they learn war any more.

THE END

INDEX